BEGINNER'S GUIDE TO
Coin Collecting

BEGINNER'S GUIDE TO

Coin Collecting

HOWARD LINECAR

LONDON
PELHAM BOOKS

First published in Great Britain by
PELHAM BOOKS LTD
26 Bloomsbury Street
*London, W.C.*1
SEPTEMBER 1966
SECOND IMPRESSION OCTOBER 1966
THIRD IMPRESSION DECEMBER 1966

Set and printed in Great Britain by Tonbridge Printers,
Ltd, Peach Hall Works, Tonbridge, Kent, in Bell eleven on
thirteen point, on paper made by Henry Bruce at Currie,
Midlothian, and bound by James Burn at Esher, Surrey

For Sarah Griffin

Acknowledgments

I am most grateful to the Keeper of Coins and Medals, British Museum, for permission to illustrate many of the coins in his care, and to Keith Howes for making the many plaster casts, including some of coins in his own collection.

I am also greatly obliged to Miss Anne S. Robertson, of Glasgow University, Miss E. M. Shaw of the South African Museum, C. Wilson Peck, lately President of the British Numismatic Society, R. S. Yeoman, J. E. Charlton and the editors of Cunobelin and Numismatic Literature for permission to quote from their published works. Also to E. C. Joslin for help and advice on the section on decorations, to Miss P. K. McCawley for typing the manuscript, to Messrs. A. C. Cooper, who took many of the photographs, and to Messrs. Spink & Son, in whose employment I have learned what little I know about so large a subject.

Finally I must thank the large number of collectors, artists, coin dealers, authors, museum curators, librarians and many others the world over with whom I have come into contact over the last 30 years. They have all in a thousand different ways taught me something about coins, medals, collecting, numismatic appreciation and authorship. My thanks to them all.

Contents

Illustrations

facing page 32

1. In the beginning coins were roughly shaped lumps of metal. This piece from Ionia is made of electrum ('white gold') and was struck before 700 B.C. (In the British Museum).

2. A particularly beautiful Ancient Greek coin. A silver 10 drachm of Akragas, struck about 408 B.C. Obverse, the Chariot of Helios (the sun), sometimes called a quadriga: four horses. Reverse: two eagles carrying off a hare. Note the grasshopper (or locust) in the background. Each side of the coin was probably the work of a separate artist. Such is frequently the case with coins down to the present time. (In the British Museum).

3. A Roman coin, struck in Britain.

4. A Byzantine gold solidus. Note the seated figure of Christ on the reverse.

5. The British Sovereign. Struck in 1964, the reverse is still based on that of the first modern Sovereign, the original design being by Pistrucci. It was first used in this form on British coinage in 1817.

6. The British Crown. This example was struck in 1953 to mark the coronation of Elizabeth II. Made of cupro-nickel.

7. The original British silver Florin of 1849. The obverse legend omitted the abbreviation D.G. (= by the Grace of God (I reign)). This led to a storm of protest. The piece was later replaced by the 'Gothic' Florin, illustrated later.

8. The Shilling. The obverse is common to the English Shilling, (reverse three leopards (not lions)) and the Scottish Shilling (reverse the lion of Scotland).

9

Illustrations

9. A set of Maundy Money, 1963. The obverse is common to the 4d., 3d., 2d., and 1d. These pieces, which are current coin of the realm, are the only silver coins at present struck in the British series. They are one of the world's smallest issues, less than 2,000 of each piece being struck each year.

10. An English hammered Penny. Known as the 'long cross' type by reason of the extent of the cross on the reverse. The obverse legend, HENRICVS REX III dates the piece as being struck in the mid-thirteenth century. Further close study of the smaller points of the design would place the piece in one of seven groups. The name of the moneyer (the person striking the piece) and the town of issue form the reverse legend. A little study will show that the lettering and even the face itself are made up from a number of standard shapes, just as children today make up pictures from a number of coloured standard shapes of paper.

facing page 33

11. The complete range of British coinage, struck as a proof set in 1937 to mark the coronation of George VI. The small case contains the £5, £2, Sovereign (£1) and Half Sovereign (10s.) in gold, and the larger case all the remaining denominations from Crown to Farthing, including the four Maundy pieces. At this time all the white pieces were struck in silver.

12. A coin auction sale in progress in Messrs. Glendining's rooms in London. The buyers at the table come from all over the world.

facing page 48

13. A modern, uncirculated, machine-produced British Crown, 1965. The areas marked show places where the coin has sustained damage either before it left the Royal Mint or afterwards by being shaken up in a bag with many other pieces. It is still, strictly speaking, in mint state.

14. An Anglo-Saxon Sceatta, showing on the reverse a charming little dragon. Dragons appear so frequently on coins that one could almost believe of some substance in the legend of their existence. (Coin in the British Museum).

15. The dodecagonal (12-sided) Threepence as it was first put into circulation in 1937.

16. A Maria Theresa Thaler. Though dated 1780, this piece was struck in the 1960's.

17. The Canadian Dollar of 1949, showing a ship. Struck to commemorate the Federation of Newfoundland with Canada in that year. The ship is the *Matthew* of John Cabot, so far as its appearance is now known. A Venetian merchant who settled in Bristol, Cabot set off in 1497 to discover the North-West Passage to India. Instead he discovered Newfoundland and the mainland of America, a year before Columbus discovered the West Indies. Such an event is worthy of commemoration on the most durable of all records, a coin.

18. A set of Irish coinage. The obverse, the harp, is common to all the denominations from Halfcrown to Farthing. All the reverses show local fauna.

facing page 49

19. A 'double' transparent plastic envelope, in which both the coin and its description can be seen. A manilla envelope, made from special dry paper, to hold a coin.

20. A 'knife box' with coins in ranked envelops. An inexpensive but rather unsatisfactory method of keeping a coin collection. It is mainly useful for the collector who travels considerably and must either put his collection in a safe deposit or take it with him with a view to adding to it on his travels.

21. The beautiful built-in coin cabinet by Chippendale, at Nostell Priory, Yorkshire.

facing page 64

22 and 22a.

A modern coin cabinet.

23. A coin album.

24. A box-file cabinet.

facing page 65

25. The 50 Lepta of Modern Greece. A cupro-nickel piece, the obverse design looks back to great days of coin artistry in Ancient Greece. The sardonic smile on the face of a one-time Greek Goddess seems to ask: to what base uses are we descended?

26. The gold 10 Francs of the now tourist state of Liechtenstein, one of the sole remaining states of those into which much of Europe was once divided.

27. The aluminium-bronze 2 Franc piece of the 'golden' state of Monaco.

28. The silver Rouble struck to commemorate the 300th anniversary of the Romanoff Regime in Russia, a regime so soon afterwards to be swept from all but the pages of history.

29. The bronze One Cent piece of Sarawak, symbolic of the White Rajah, Malayan pirates and European 'progress' brought to the Far East.

30. One of the relatively few square coins issued for general circulation, the bronze One Cent piece of the then Straits Settlements, 1926.

31. The end of an Empire. The last type of Rupee, cupro-nickel, issued under British rule in India. It replaced a long series of silver Rupees, similar to number 32.

33. The first separate coinage of Southern Rhodesia is typified in the silver Half Crown of 1932.

facing page 80

34. The silver proof Crown of New Zealand, 1935. Known as the 'Waitangi Crown' by reason of the reverse design: Captain Hobson shaking hands with a Maori Chief: this first Crown piece marked the Jubilee of George V, not the centenary of the signing of the Treaty of Waitangi in 1840. This latter event was commemorated by a special Half Crown, struck in 1940.

35. Not as old as it looks. This 50 Mazuna piece of Morocco was not struck in A.D. 1289.

36. Another unusual shape for a coin issued for general circulation. A cupro-nickel Ten Cents of the Seychelles, 1939. Such a piece is usually described as having a serrated edge.

37. The first silver Dollar issued for circulation in Canada, 1935. Though such a Dollar had been designed in 1911, and is illustrated on another plate, this was the first issued for currency. Till then the Dollar was a 'paper name'. The 1935 Dollar marked the Jubilee of George V.

38. A group of four token coins, typical of a large series in use in Canada before a coinage was struck for the Dominion as one whole country. The first of the latter pieces are dated 1858–9.

Illustrations

39. The coin that never appeared in circulation. A silver proof of the design for the Canadian Dollar of 1911, one of the rarest of the modern coins in the world, so far as is at present known.

40. The silver Fourpence or Groat, struck at the Royal Mint for use in far-away British Guiana.

41. The first British attempt at a decimal coinage, referred to earlier, was to have repercussions half a world away. The Florin, as used in the Fiji Islands.

42. The coinage of a king who never was crowned. The first piece to reach Europe was the bronze Penny of New Guinea.

43. It was closely followed by the cupro-nickel Penny, Halfpenny and One Tenth Penny of British West Africa, and by the bronze Ten and Five cents of East Africa (not illustrated, but similar in appearance). It is said that the Tenth Penny is often used as a washer, since washers cost at least a half-penny. In what places, then, will this little coin be found one hundred years from now?

44. William Wyon's magnificent design for a Five Pound, or Crown, piece of Queen Victoria, 1839. Usually known as the 'Una and the Lion', the reverse shows Victoria as Una, guiding the British Lion. It is said that the design was not accepted since it was thought to be too medallic. Remembering what has been said about the way in which coins are damaged almost before they leave the mint, the beautiful high relief of the reverse would certainly soon have been spoiled had the piece been put into general circulation.

45. Few pattern pieces exist in the British series before 1662, when the whole coinage was redesigned and produced by primitive machinery. This pattern crown of 1663 is another design that was never put into production for a coin for general use, though it is very similar to the design actually accepted. The piece illustrated was designed by Thomas Simon, and the edge, which defies illustration, was inscribed with the legend, THOMAS SIMON MOST HUMBLY PRAYS YOUR MAJESTY TO COMPARE THIS HIS TRYALL PIECE WITH THE DUTCH AND AND IF MORE TRULY DRAWN AND EMBOSSED MORE GRACE-FULLY ORDERED AND MORE ACCURATELY ENGRAVED TO

13

RELIEVE HIM. This long legend was placed in two lines round the thin edge of the coin, itself a triumph, bearing in mind the mechanical facilities of the period. It was Simon's protest against the designs for the new milled coinage being accepted from a Dutch artist, Roettier. In modern parlance, it was a similar situation to that of a British firm losing a contract to a Dutch firm for, say, the designs for all British power stations for the next 30 years.

46. Very many designs seem to have been considered before the so-called 'Gothic' Florin (here illustrated) was accepted. After the 'Godless' Florin, already illustrated, this piece went into general circulation, and ousted the Half Crown for some 20 years. An enlarged and even more complex version of the 'Gothic' Florin theme became the 'Gothic' Crown, which probably never circulated. The many pattern Florins struck from designs not accepted could, and have, formed a fine and valuable collection of themselves.

47. The Crown of 1951. Struck to mark the centenary of the Great Exhibition of 1851, the Festival of Britain of 1951 and the 400th anniversary of the first English silver Crown of 1551. Some of these Crowns were struck at a Branch Mint on South Bank, then the Festival site, at about where the north-eastern part of the Shell Centre now stands. The pieces struck there have, unfortunately, no distinguishing mark. They were carefully struck and could be classified as proofs. In the light of later events, referred to in the text, they are probably more accurately classified as specimen pieces.

48. In more recent times a new class of piece, neither proof nor pattern, has been struck in the British Commonwealth. This 1965 Canadian Dollar is an example of such a piece. Carefully struck and highly polished, it contains none of the blemishes shown on the 'Churchill' Crown previously illustrated. One would have thought that the great leader was worthy of no less consideration. To such pieces as this Dollar the term 'Specimen' has come into use as a term of condition description. The 1951 Crown just illustrated might also be placed in this category.

49. For the Trade Fair, held in New York in 1960, Crowns were struck at the Royal Mint on Tower Hill and exported. This is one of the pieces. Its design is that intended for use when ever a Crown piece might be struck after the coronation,

14

which was commemorated by its own special design, previously illustrated.

facing page 97

50. The large Roman gold medallion, part of the famous Arras Treasure. The pictorial scene on the reverse is of the greatest interest. The technical skill needed to produce so fine a piece about 2,000 years ago is quite remarkable. Note the 'White Tower' on the left.

51. The not very imaginative design of the last of a long line of official Coronation Medals which started with James I, 1603–1625. This piece was struck for the coronation of George VI, and was offered in two sizes (of which this is the smaller), and three metals, gold, silver and bronze.

52. A crown piece, struck from the silver captured at the Battle of Vigo Bay, 1702. Note the word VIGO below the bust of Queen Anne.

facing page 112

53. When we come to such events as the building of our railways we often find detailed pictorial representations of such engineering achievements. This is one of several medals struck to commemorate the opening of the Liverpool and Manchester Railway, 1830. What ever may be said about the work of that tough old Northumbrian George Stephenson, the Liverpool and Manchester Railway was his personal achievement. With little or no education by modern standards, but with a vast reservoir of sound common sense, 'Old George' set the standard for the steam operated railways of the world. The minute detail shown on the reverse of this medal is typical of the 'picture medal' of the period.

54. Sir Isambart Marc Brunel, F.R.S., the man who started to dig the world's first underwater tunnel, which is still in use, beneath the River Thames. The reverse of this pictorial medal shows a section of the bore. Twenty years in the building, owing mainly to lack of text-book knowledge: the text-books not yet having been written: this pioneer tunnel was completed by Marc's son, I. K. Brunel, the most flamboyant of the Victorian railway engineers. 'I.K.' built the Clifton suspension bridge, the Great Western Railway, the *Great Eastern* (a ship far in advance of her time), and other

Victorian engineering marvels. He also swallowed a Sovereign by accident while entertaining children with a conjuring trick, and invented, on the spot, a method of recovering it before its presence could cause his death.

55. A modern commemorative medal, struck to mark the 50th anniversary of the building of the Simplon Tunnel. The obverse represents the efforts of the workers, hewing a tunnel through solid Alpine rock, while the reverse shows one of the portals of the tunnel.

facing page 113

56. Commemorative medals have been given as awards. Such are Davison's medals. This medal is, then, something of a hybrid. It commemorates the Battle of Trafalgar, 1805, and was struck by Nelson's prize agent for those who took part in the action. Admirals received it in gold, lower ranks in silver and lower deck ratings in bronze; who mostly scorned it and threw it overboard. Had it been given attached to a brooch and riband in the modern style they would probably have worn their 'decoration' with pride.

57. 'The earliest instance we know of one (medal) commemorative of a particular event being evidently meant to be worn as an ornament is the Armada Medal'. Attached to a riband or silken cord it could be worn as a 'dress ornament'; a 'decoration'; just as today our ladies are liable to wear a clutch of gold coins or ornaments attached to a bracelet. Herein lies the origin of our modern system of military and civil decorations and awards. In another 400 years what will our present ladies' bracelets have become?

58. Awarded for academic achievement. The obverse of the gold Sanford Saltus medal, awarded every three years by the British Numismatic Society for outstanding contribution to the science of numismatics. The reverse is engraved with the recipient's name and the year of the award.

facing page 128

59. A typical group of Seventeenth Century Tokens; round, octagonal and heart-shaped.

60. A group of Eighteenth Century Tokens in the 'London Buildings' series. On the left are two typical obverse types. The reverses show, Goldsmiths Hall, as rebuilt after the

Great Fire of London, 1666, the Royal Exchange of 1669, conceived by Thomas Gresham and long since demolished; Wren's Monument to the Great Fire (he had ideas that the column might be used as a telescope: shades of Jodrell Bank!), and the Tower of London (not so unlike the fortress shown on the medallion of Constantius Chlorus?).

61. The Cornish Penny token of the Nineteenth Century series. Note the Watt beam engine on the obverse, used for driving the pumps to keep water out of the workings. Such a wood and iron engine can be seen, often working, in the Science Museum, London. The little shapes on the reverse on either side of the fish are blocks of tin and copper, then, with fishing, the staple products of Cornwall.

facing page 129

62. 'The majority of these are Spanish Eight Reale coins'. A 5s. token made from one such piece for the Deanston Cotton Mill. The figure 3 has been partly obliterated by what appears to be part of the head of George III. The basic coin was therefore probably countermarked by the Bank of England, as mentioned in the text, for use as one of their tokens for 4s. 9d.

63. A similar piece for Cromford, Derbyshire, countermarked for 4s. 9d.

64. One of the large number of Nineteenth Century silver tokens.

65. South Eastern and Chatham Railway, uniface bronze token or ticket, issued at Blackfriars Station.

66. Sheffield & Rotherham Railway bronze omnibus check, engraved with the serial number 1819.

facing page 144

67. Allied to maps, time charts, historical pictures and the like, coins can be brought to life. A method in use for displaying coins in the Stockholm Cabinet. These cases show Swedish monetary history through the ages, the story being told in gold lettering embossed on leather, placed above the frame. Throughout the Stockholm Cabinet every effort is made to display coins in such a way that they attract. Visitors are not fatigued by having to stoop, lean over horizontal

cases or fight against a back-reflection from badly designed lighting. It is worth a trip to Stockholm to see what *can* be done with a little imagination to make coins attractive. The museums of Britain lag far behind in exploring such possibilities for their collections of coins.

68. Heberden Coin Room, Ashmolean Museum, Oxford, a further fine display of coins and medals.

facing page 145

69. The 'picture medal' at its best. The hollow bronze box, shown in the middle, opens to disclose ten charming aquatints in full colour. These depict the major naval engagements of Lord Nelson, whose portrait appears on the lid of the box.

Introduction

The collecting of coins and medals as an instructive and rewarding hobby is on the increase. Interest in this subject has never been so high. The formation of such a collection as an investment of capital also increases year by year. Properly built, a coin or medal collection will prove a sound investment. This has been illustrated over many centuries. Coin collecting goes back in time for many hundreds of years.

How coins and medals are, or should be, collected requires some little guidance. There have been those who have ventured into the unknown field of numismatics only to their regret. This should not be.

This book is written to help those who would take an interest in coin collecting correctly to appreciate its various facets. It is not difficult to write a dogmatic book telling the beginner what he should collect and how he should go about it. In this book the subject is approached from a somewhat different angle.

In writing this *Beginner's Guide to Coin Collecting* the author is attempting, through the written word, to extend a friendly hand to his readers: to those who are prepared to join with him in exploring what coin collecting is all about. He is not setting himself up as an authority on the subject. After some thirty years in the business of caring for and trying to advise coin collectors, he knows that he still has very much to learn.

CHAPTER ONE

Some Thoughts on what Coins to Collect

We are constantly reminded that this is the age of the specialist. This can also apply to coin collecting. With a few exceptions a vast collection of coins, containing something of everything, is a collection of the past. Only a very rich collector could, in any age, form such a coin collection. Though rewarding by its very richness and variety, a lifetime of leisure is necessary for the true appreciation of such a collection. One or two such magnificent collections will be mentioned, together with the use to which they were eventually put.

Not so long ago coin collecting was looked upon as a rich man's hobby and as something of the preserve of the historian and of the student. Now, with the somewhat more even distribution of money, with the greater freedom afforded by modern civilisation and, more particularly, with the higher standard of general education, more people are able to join the ranks of coin collectors. They, in their turn, by specialisation, are getting more from their collections.

Today we have the specialist who, following a line of individual interest, builds up a relatively small collection, studies it, and obtains from it the utmost knowledge and interest that it can provide. By so doing the collector adds to his own mental stature, enjoys his collection to the full, and can speak with certainty on its content to other collectors. How this last observation applies will be seen in a chapter which follows.

In the beginning quite often a handful of apparently

worthless coins will start a collector. Something among them fires his imagination. He begins to ask questions about some of the coins, to follow up some line of thought. At once he becomes a collector in embryo. If he now considers his miscellaneous handful of coins with more care, begins to look about for the chance of adding to those which interest him and to discard those which do not, he has become a collector.

It is probably true to say that there are relatively few cases of a person who, seeing such a book as this offered, will buy it, read it, and then say to himself, 'I will become a coin collector.' Of course such instances do occur, but in the main the spark of interest comes from the coins themselves: from the miscellaneous handful mentioned above, from the odd strange coins that fall into the hand, or from many similar instances. Just as one may buy a book on railways, having found interest in trains at a station, or a book on aircraft, having seen aeroplanes come and go at an airport, so the average collector receives his inspiration to collect from coins themselves rather than from reading about them.

Since coins have been in use for some 2,000 years, the line of interest which the collector may follow through the numismatic maze, once the spark of interest has flashed in his mind, is known to him alone. The course which he will follow can only depend on what the individual saw for a brief moment in the flash of that spark of interest. Even then the collector may proceed vaguely at first. Collections develop with the collector, are governed by the money available, by opportunity, and by many similar factors. In trying to be of some help on what to collect, therefore, some very general thought on the subject and some fairly broad treatment of it may find an answering thought in the potential collector's mind. As stated above, the potential collector may only come across this book after his appetite has been whetted.

Bearing all this in mind, as an introduction to the subject of coins and coin collecting it may be of some help to break up the whole subject into a number of large groups. It is an historical fact that some countries had become highly civilised before coins were evolved. The ancient Egyptians had no coins as we know them, yet their civilisation was of a very high order. There were quite a few other groups of people who, in more recent times, contrived to live without coins, mainly because they were self-centred, and had little contact with the outside world. Reference will be made to this point later.

It fell to the Ancient Greeks to evolve the beginnings of coinage as we know it today. This evolution took place some 700 years B.C. In the beginning their coins were roughly shaped lumps of metal, stamped with some recognisable sign. So stamped they could be accepted as a piece of metal of known weight and value, and were a promise that such pieces of metal could at any time be exchanged for goods: basically food and other necessities of life: to be obtained from the person who had issued these pieces of metal.

Modern coins are no more than this; a promise to redeem in goods. Only their form and the exactness of their shape and weight has changed. It is a basic fact in economics that money is only a promise to pay.

Between 700 B.C. and the rise of the Roman Empire to domination in the Mediterranean area the Greeks brought an increasing degree of importance to such metal stamping: to coin making. The first crude recognisable marks on roughly shaped pieces of metal evolved into the heads of deities and animals, associated with the place or person issuing the coin.

It should be remembered that Ancient Greece was a collection of City States. Just as the Greater London Council now rules a large metropolitan area: just as the many County Boroughs of Britain administer territorial areas within the country, so in Ancient Greece each City State was sufficient unto itself. The main numismatic difference is that our British coinage emanates from one Mint alone though, as will be stated, this was not always so.

As coins evolved from the private issues of the Ancient Greek traders, so the City States began to issue their own coinage. Such coins, of known value, began to be acceptable between the City States just as now various coinages are acceptable between various countries at determined rates of exchange. Such exchanges of coinage are not new. Only the picture grows in size as civilisation advances.

Many of the coins which survive from the Ancient Greek period have never been surpassed in artistic merit. In these remote times such coins were not issued in the millions in which coins are struck today, nor were they in the hands of the population as a whole for daily use.

It is, therefore, a fact that the study and appreciation of Ancient Greek coins is something of a subject apart, not only among collectors but from a book such as this. They are relatively expensive to collect and need some knowledge of Greek history and of the Greek language. But they are by no means a 'closed shop' to the beginner. He may well have an interest in Ancient Greece and the spread of its civilisation: he may well 'graduate' in this interest as his collecting interest grows.

In the numismatic sequence of history the Greek civilisation was followed by that of the Romans. In Roman times the issue of coins became more prolific. As Roman influence expanded over the then known world, more and more money was needed to keep the Roman world going. Gold, silver, and bronze coins were issued, as they had been in Ancient Greece. As Roman economic tides rose and fell, so their coinage was either genuine gold and silver, or debased: base metal pieces 'washed' over with gold and silver. Plating had not then been invented. This debasement of the coinage occurs again and again throughout history. Our own 'silver' coins are in reality only made of a combination of copper and nickel.

The coins issued by the Romans spread to wherever the Roman legions penetrated. They might not be accepted by the 'uncivilised' people which the Romans conquered, but the legionaires themselves had to be paid in coins which they knew and would accept. Thus we find Roman coins in use as far apart as Asia and Great Britain. Some Roman coins were actually struck in Britain. Hoards of Roman coins frequently come to light under the plough of the British farmer, or under the excavator of the modern builder.

Just as the Ancient Greeks portrayed gods, goddesses and animals on their coins, as recognition symbols of the various Greek City States, the Romans portrayed their Emperors and rulers. It is, therefore, possible to study the portraits of the Caesars and other great men of their day on the coins of the Roman period. This fact in itself gives a possible line of specialisation for the collector who has an interest in Roman history. Most children learn something, however brief, of this history at school. Roman coins can help to bring this history to life. The people whose heads are shown on Roman coins really lived and breathed. They are not mere fiction, or names in a history book.

Even so, the man with a miscellaneous collection of 'modern' coins in his hand may feel that this is all rather remote. But all this is the story of money as we now know it and as such should be followed through so that it can be seen where our modern money came from.

Broadly then, Roman coins fall into three parts: those of the Roman Empire period; those of the Roman Republican period, when Roman Emperors were rulers of the past and democracy prevailed; and the coinage of Byzantium, the Eastern Roman Empire based on Constantinople: Istanbul in modern geography; the period when the once great Roman Empire was gradually crumbling to final extinction, as many empires since have crumbled.

This latter series of coins, generally known as the Byzantine series, a series in which gold coins are relatively speaking common, reflects all the richness and affluence of the gradually disintegrating Roman world. It also reflects the rise of Christianity, the conversion of many Byzantine rulers to that faith, and the beginnings of rule by humanity rather than by armed force.

Thus the whole Roman series of coins are packed with interest, colour and history. The series are catalogued variously, from the most erudite works running into many volumes, to the handy guide, helpful to the beginner who may choose this as his line of specialisation. Reference to such catalogues and guides is given in the bibliography. The Roman series is, therefore, one which any collector may tackle, and a series of coins from which he can gain much interest and knowledge.

It may be gleaned from what has been said that Greek coinage was on a local basis, centred on the Greek City States. It may reasonably be said of the Romans that they introduced coinage to the western world, which then consisted of Europe and what was known of Asia and Africa. To the Romans this was 'the world', though they were shrewd enough, as had been the Egyptians and Greeks before them, to realise that the world which they knew was not by any means all that could be discovered.

Thus, the Romans spread civilisation as far over the earth's surface as they could penetrate while still able to keep their supply lines going. As civilisation spread the core of the Roman world gradually disintegrated. They left their mark on many countries which, in turn, began to rise in the civilisation scale. With such rise came coinage as a means of facilitating trade and progress, slowly though these may have developed. Roman coins were as a stone dropped into a still pool. The ripples spread slowly outward till they lapped at last on shores the Romans never knew.

Now, therefore, comes a point of departure. There now has to be considered each country as it evolved its civilisation and development, each country's coinage evolving with it.

As such countries came and went across the pages of time, amalgamated with or were conquered by other countries, so the coinage picture became bigger and more complex, and thus more and more interesting. By a thousand small steps the world of today emerged; a world divided into a reasonably small number of territorial areas. These areas may seem numerically large. By comparison it has to be remembered that Europe, as an example, was once divided into many small states, and that each such state was likely to have its own local coinage. So an immense and complex numismatic picture begins to evolve. On top of this came the discovery, so far as Europe was concerned, of the New World and the world of the Far East in which China had evolved a system of money as long ago as Roman times. Now the numismatic picture is really large. It will at once be appreciated how great are the interests that lie before the coin collector.

Indeed so large is the picture that the potential collector may well feel that he is facing something quite incomprehensible. In the very size of the picture lies the germ of specialisation which may well set the collector along his own particular line. Beyond his own particular line of interest the collector need not penetrate the numismatic jungle any further, and along his own particular line there are works of reference to help. More will be said of them later.

So much emphasis has been placed on specialisation that it might appear that this is the be-all and end-all of coin collecting. This is not so. Though a highly specialised collection is rewarding to the serious student, there are many collectors who enjoy a more general collection of coins. Even so a theme of collecting interest generally runs through the collection.

What has been said so far may have tended to magnify the numismatic picture out of reasonable proportion. Lest the potential collector be frightened off the subject, the next chapter will deal with something more specific.

CHAPTER TWO

Something about British coinage

An obvious line of interest for the British collector lies in the study of British coins. The same may be said of the collector in any other country. The coins which are in every day use in Britain have a very long and interesting history, and about these coins many stories can be told.

Since the more familiar coins in day to day use are but a part of the British series as a whole, it should perhaps be pointed out that there are, in theory, three series of coins in use. These series are struck in gold, silver, now cupro-nickel, and bronze.

Of the first metal, gold, no coins are now in circulation, though the theoretical basis of our coinage is still the gold pound or Sovereign. Of true silver coins there are now but four denominations still struck. These are a separate small series which will be detailed in a moment. The mass of 'silver' coins which pass through our hands every day are, in reality, made of a blend of copper and nickel, known as cupro-nickel. Of bronze coins there are but three left, the penny and the halfpenny, and, for purposes of classification, the twelve-sided threepence, though this latter piece is actually struck in nickel-brass, another blending of two metals.

Since the 'silver' range of coins is the most familiar their story will be given first. The unit of the range is the Crown, or five-shilling piece. This is rarely seen in actual use. This is partly because it is a rather large and heavy coin, $1\frac{1}{2}$ inches in diameter, and thus somewhat cumbersome to carry in any quantity. It is still, however, the 'head' of the 'silver coinage', and more detail will be given about it in a moment.

Next comes the half-crown, an obvious division of the Crown and a coin familiar by its millions, the largest coin in every day use. Next down the scale is the Florin, or two-shilling piece, equally familiar. A moment's reflection will show that this piece is not a logical sub-division of the Crown or five shillings. In fact it is a mathematical sub-division of the pound. Since the pound, or Sovereign, is composed of twenty shillings (or four Crowns), the Florin or two shillings is one-tenth part of a pound. This gives rise to thoughts about decimal coinage, and there is obviously a story which is worth telling concerning the Florin.

In fact the Florin had its origins in a Victorian attempt to decimalise British coinage. The decimal system as a whole had its origins in the 18th century, and the present suggestion that British coinage should be placed on a decimal basis is not new. In the event attempts to place British coinage on a decimal basis in the reign of Victoria (1837–1901) got no further than some lengthy official reports, the preparation of a number of pattern pieces for such a coinage, and the introduction of the Florin in 1849, as the one-tenth of a pound. It should be recalled that at this period the gold Sovereign, or pound piece, was in daily circulation and that the Bank of England Pound Note, now so familiar, had still to replace the gold Sovereign in daily use.

With the introduction of the Florin, the conversion of British coinage to a decimal basis stopped. One of the results of the introduction of the new piece was that for some years after its appearance the issue of half-Crowns was suspended.

Next in value to the Florin down the scale is the Shilling. This coin now has two distinct designs, the English shilling and the Scottish. The latter has no reference to territory but was introduced in 1937, the first year of the coinage of the reign of George VI, as a compliment to the Queen Consort, the lady who is now Queen Elizabeth the Queen Mother.

The illustrations of the two pieces show how distinct they are, though it is a fact that many people fail to notice this point.

The smallest of our normal 'silver' coins is the sixpence, the half of the shilling. Below this value comes the nickel-brass twelve-sided threepence, and the bronze Penny and Halfpenny. Till recent years there was also a bronze Farthing, the fourth part of a Penny. The issue of this little piece was discontinued many years after it had no purchasing power of its own, and when the cost of striking it exceeded its face value. It was demonitised, that is declared no longer of legal tender, in 1963.

Additional to these, our very familiar coins, are a small and very interesting set of four pieces, now known as Maundy Money. Here is another story which it is worth digressing to record.

This little set of coins consist of a Fourpence, Threepence, Twopence and Penny. While all our other 'silver' coins are now made of cupro-nickel, these four pieces alone are still struck in silver. They are now issued only as Royal Maundy Money, for distribution to a number of Royal Pensioners every Maundy Thursday. How they fit into our coinage will be shown in a moment in the more concise 'family tree' of coinage which will follow. Their actual use is of interest.

A list of Royal Pensioners is kept by the Royal Almonry at Buckingham Palace. Broadly, anyone who has been an employer of labour and who now exists on small means can apply, usually through their parish priest for possible inclusion.

Each Maundy Thursday a special service is held in one of our abbeys or cathedrals. Formerly this service had been held in Westminster Abbey for very many years, but in the present reign it has been held in other cities than Westminster. Her Majesty Queen Elizabeth II has attended the service whenever possible and has distributed the Royal Maundy to the pensioners in person.

As many men and as many women as the Queen has years

of age each receive as many pence as the Queen's years total. They also receive additional money in place of food and clothing which were once distributed in kind. A little calculation will soon show that, if the Queen be 40 years of age, each pensioner receives four sets of coins, consisting of Penny, Twopence, Threepence and Fourpence. As these coins total ten pence in face value, the Maundy series is a little decimal system on its own and is easily adapted to any number of pence, as required by the Sovereign's age.

If the calculation is carried through, in the case in point, it will be seen that 80 pensioners each receive 16 coins, a total of 1,280 pieces. Certain persons who officiate at the annual service also receive one set of four pieces, a traditional method of payment for their help. Such persons are relatively few in number so it will at once be seen that the Royal Maundy Money pieces are one of the world's smallest issues. They are therefore much prized by collectors. As stated above, they are the last four coins in the British series that are still struck in silver.

Naturally there is much more history behind the Maundy ceremony than is given in this short account. The origins of the custom are not completely known, but the story can be found in full in a little book called *The Royal Maundy*, which can be obtained from the Royal Almonry, Buckingham Palace (2s. 6d.). The proceeds from the sale of this book are devoted to charity. It is despatched in an envelope post marked 'Buckingham Palace', a cover not without interest to collectors in another field.

To return to the family tree of our British coinage. Nothing so far has been said in any detail about gold coinage. Most of us have heard of the Sovereign, though probably few have ever seen this coin. Though the Sovereign has been struck during the present reign it cannot be put into circulation. This is because the amount of gold which it contains, worth some £3 12s. 0d., is greatly in excess of its face value of £1 0s. 0d.

There are several reasons why, after a very long interval, Sovereigns have again been struck at the Royal Mint. It is not only useful to keep the mint operatives familiar with the striking of gold coins, a process which needs its own particular skill, but it is a fact that in certain parts of the East the British Sovereign is still used since it is of a known weight, fineness and value. In such countries people often keep considerable sums of money in British Sovereigns.

1 In the beginning coins were roughly shaped lumps of metal. This piece from Ionia is made of electrum ('white gold') and was struck before 700 B.C. (In the British Museum). **2** A particularly beautiful Ancient Greek coin. A silver 10 drachm of Akragas, struck about 408 B.C. Obverse, the Chariot of Helios (the sun), sometimes called a quadriga: four horses. Reverse: two eagles carrying off a hare. Note the grasshopper (or locust) in the background. Each side of the coin was probably the work of a separate artist. Such is frequently the case with coins down to the present time. (In the British Museum). **3** A Roman coin, struck in Britain. **4** A Byzantine gold solidus. Note the seated figure of Christ on the reverse. **5** The British Sovereign. Struck in 1964, the reverse is still based on that of the first modern Sovereign, the original design being by Pistrucci. It was first used in this form on British coinage in 1817. **6** The British Crown. This example was struck in 1953 to mark the coronation of Elizabeth II. Made of cupronickel. **7** The original British silver Florin of 1849. The obverse legend omitted the abbreviation D.G. (=by the Grace of God (Ireign)) This led to a storm of protest. The piece was later replaced by the 'Gothic' Florin, illustrated later. **8** The Shilling. The obverse is common to the English Shilling (reverse three leopards (not lions)), and the Scottish Shilling (reverse the lion of Scotland). **9** A set of Maundy Money, 1963. The obverse is common to the 4d., 3d., 2d., and 1d. These pieces, which are current coin of the realm, are the only silver coins at present struck in the British series. They are one of the world's smallest issues, less than 2,000 of each piece being struck each year. **10** An English hammered Penny. Known as the 'long cross' type by reason of the extent of the cross on the reverse. The obverse legend, HENRICVS REX III dates the piece as being struck in the mid-thirteenth century. Further close study of the smaller points of the design would place the piece in one of seven groups. The name of the moneyer (the person striking the piece) and the town of issue form the reverse legend. A little study will show that the lettering and even the face itself are made up from a number of standard shapes, just as children today make up pictures from a number of coloured standard shapes of paper

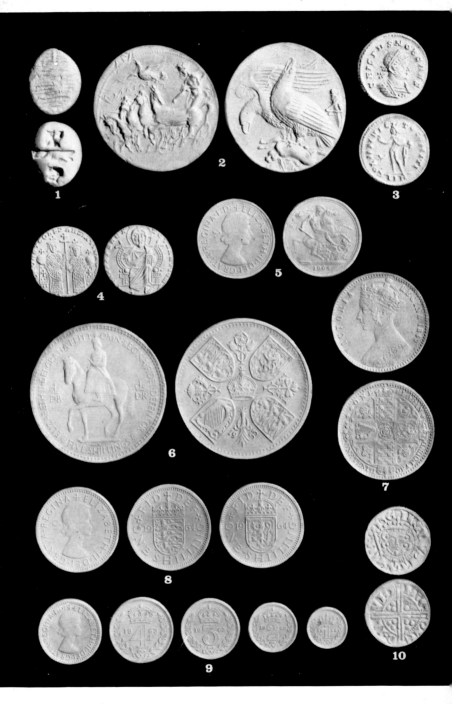

11 The complete range of British coinage, struck as a proof set in 1937 to mark the coronation of George VI. The small case contains the £5, £2, Sovereign (£1) and Half Sovereign (10s.) in gold, and the larger case all the remaining denominations from Crown to Farthing, including the four Maundy pieces. At this time all the white pieces were struck in silver. (Photo: courtesy of Messrs. Spink and Son)

12 A coin auction sale in progress in Messrs. Glendining's rooms in London. The buyers at the table come from all over the world. (Photo: courtesy of D. J. Crowther Ltd.)

From the time when the Sovereign in its present form was first struck, 1817, there has always been a Half-Sovereign, though the striking of this piece was not resumed when Sovereigns were struck in the present reign. At various times Five- and Two-Pound pieces have also been struck in gold. It is doubtful if they were ever used in general circulation.

Probably the simplest way in which to explain this and other points about our coinage is to set down the family tree in full, with some notes as to the origins of the pieces which are or were in normal circulation. This family tree looks something like this:

GOLD

Five Pounds. First struck as a proof piece in the reign of George III, (1760–1820), and occasionally struck since, usually at Coronations or Royal Jubilees, down to the present reign, of which two pieces are known, one in the Royal Collection, Windsor Castle, the other in the British Museum. There is probably a third in the Royal Mint Museum. A descendent of the Five-Guinea piece, first struck in the reign of Charles II (1660–1685).

Two Pounds. First struck as a proof in the reign of George IV (1820–1830) and also as a piece for general use. The name Double Sovereign goes back to Henry VIII (1509–1547). Occasionally struck since, usually as for the £5-piece. A descendent of the Two-Guinea piece, introduced with the £5 5s. 0d.

Sovereign or Pound Piece. First struck in its present form in the reign of George III, in 1817, though the name goes back to Henry VII (1485–1509). The official unit of British coinage. A descendent of the Guinea, which was first struck in the reign of Charles II and took its name from the source of its metal, Guinea and the Gold Coast of Africa.

Half-Sovereign or Ten-Shilling Piece. First struck in its present form in 1817, as above, though the name goes back to Henry VII. The descendent of the Half-Guinea, which first appeared with the Guinea, as above.

SILVER AND CUPRO-NICKEL

Crown or Five-Shilling Piece. First struck as a silver piece in the reign of Edward VI (1547–1553), in the year 1551, though the name goes back to Henry VIII, where used for a gold piece. Struck fairly regularly since, especially during the reign of Victoria (1837–1901). Last struck in silver in 1937 and in cupro-nickel in 1960. The next striking was the Sir Winston Churchill commemorative Crown, dated 1965.

Half-Crown. First struck in its present form in the reign of Edward VI, when both gold and silver Half-Crowns appeared. Struck for almost every reign since. Changed to cupro-nickel (cu-ni.) 1947.

Florin, or Two-Shilling Piece. First struck in its present form in the reign of Victoria, though the name goes back to a gold coin of Edward III (1327–1377) whence it was obtained from a gold coin struck in Florence, in Italy. First struck as a tenth of a pound in 1849. Issued regularly ever since. Changed to cu-ni 1947.

Shilling. First struck as a silver piece in the reign of Henry VII. Sometime called a Testoon. Struck in almost every reign since. Changed to cu-ni 1947.

Shilling (Scottish). First issued in its present form in 1937. Struck regularly ever since in about equal numbers with the Shilling (English). Changed to cu-ni 1947. When Scotland had its own separate coinage (till the reign of Anne, (1702–1714) there was a shilling among the denominations.

Sixpence. First struck in the reign of Edward VI. Struck for almost every reign since. Changed to cu-ni 1947.

Fourpence. Probably first called 'fourpence' when issued for general circulation at the instigation of Sir Joseph Hume in 1838. Its real name is the Groat (or Great Piece) as which it was first issued in the reign of Edward III (1327–1377).

Issued regularly since. Survives as a silver piece in the Maundy Money, and is legal tender. Never issued in cu-ni.
Threepence. First struck in the reign of Edward VI. Struck regularly in almost every reign since. Disappeared from normal circulation in 1946, though still issued annually for Maundy Money and is legal tender. Never struck in cu-ni.
Two Pence. Properly called the Half Groat. Details as Groat of Edward III above.
Penny. First issued as a silver piece about 765. Issued regularly since. Survives as a silver piece in the Maundy Money and is legal tender. Never struck in cu-ni.

NICKEL-BRASS
Threepence. First issued in 1937. Struck regularly ever since.

COPPER AND BRONZE
Penny. First issued in copper in 1797. Changed to bronze 1860. Issued regularly since introduction in this metal, some few years being missed here and there.
Halfpenny. First issued in copper in about 1672. Has been struck in tin. Issued fairly consistently since, particularly after 1797. Changed to bronze 1860. Descended from a silver piece, history much as the silver penny.
Farthing. First struck under Royal Licence in the reign of James I (1603–1625). Has been issued in tin. Struck fairly regularly since, especially after 1797. Changed to bronze 1860. Demonetized 1963. Descended from a silver coin first issued in the reign of Edward I (1272–1307).

It will be seen how old are the names for some of our coins. It would be a pity to lose them all under decimalisation. It will also be seen what history and interest lie ahead of the collector of nothing more than a single denomination of our own British coinage.

It will doubtless not have escaped notice that in setting out the family tree of British coinage, reference was made to some coins which go back anything from four hundred to a thousand years. The oldest coin whose name we still use is the Penny, which, as stated, dates back to about A.D. 765. Such a long history may well give rise to the thought, what were these coins like and how were they made in times long before the invention of machinery?

The first half of our coinage, from ancient times until 1662 is quite distinct in its designs, many of its denominations, and its method of production. So far, in order to introduce coins and coin collecting from an angle that can be readily appreciated by the beginner in the subject some details have been given of coins usually classified as modern. In fact they were all produced by the rolling mill and coin press. More details of this method of production will be given later. For purposes of classification coins so produced are known as 'milled coinage'. All the more ancient countries of Europe (at least) have a coinage series known as 'hammered coinage'. This is because the coins in use were produced by the use of the hammer.

Taking our ancient English penny as an example, in its earlier history it was produced very simply. First a piece of silver was cut from a larger silver sheet. It was then carefully trimmed to the exact weight which it should have as a Penny, since coins struck in a precious metal are, as stated earlier, a known weight of that metal, hence their value. The disc of metal, roughly round in shape, was then placed between two dies. The die to produce the obverse or 'head' side is, by long tradition, always placed as the lower die, the reason being that the lower die, which does not have to take the hammer blow that is about to fall, wears the longest. As it frequently contained some attempt at a human face, such a die was more difficult to make.

The lower die having been placed firmly in a block of wood, the disc of metal was placed on it. The upper die was then placed above this and a hammer was brought smartly down on the upper die. Sometimes more than one blow was necessary. The designs on the dies were thus imprinted on the metal disc, which now became a Penny.

One or two small points arise here. It will be seen from the illustrations that few hammered coins are really round. The blow tended to spread the metal and various ideas were tried in attempts to confine this spread. It was not till a ring, known as a collar, was invented and successfully developed in the mechanical age of coin making that absolutely round coins could be produced. This spreading of the metal added to the ease with which coins could be 'clipped', that is, little pieces cut from the rough edges and saved up till a quantity of valuable metal was amassed. Penalties for clipping have always been very severe since a coinage of light weight can no longer be trusted, the ultimate result being a threat to the financial stability of the country concerned.

It has been stated that sometimes more than one blow was necessary to produce a coin. This sometimes produced what is known as 'double striking', that is, the metal or the upper die moved slightly under the rebound from the blow so that the second blow produced some parts of the design in a slightly different place. An attempt to bring down a rubber stamp twice on the same spot will produce the same effect.

Badly mis-struck coins were returned to the melting pot, just as today badly machine-made coins rarely get out of the mint. A badly struck coinage opens the door to the forger. Here again, penalties have always been heavy. A coinage containing a large number of forgeries is yet another threat to the financial stability of a country.

In fact, it is true to say that once coins had been invented and accepted in use, the whole history of money is one long attempt to produce a coinage that should not or could not be forged or clipped. Not till machine-made coins had been in use for some 200 years was it possible to make each piece absolutely round with no signs of double striking. Though exceedingly small numbers of forged coins are still made, mostly by casting, such evils are now, to all intents and purposes, things of the past. The modern forger usually turns his attention to printing false bank notes, a subject beyond the confines of this book.

A few further observations will round off this brief account of English hammered money production. The early hammered coinage of this country is always known as English hammered coinage, since our money did not become British till after the Union with Scotland. This did not take place till the reign of Anne (1702–1714), some years after milled coinage had been in use (1662).

The Pennies of long ago, which have been taken as the example, were struck at many mints all over the country. Far back in Anglo-Saxon and Norman times the ancient towns of England were very much little self-centred communities on their own. The only means of travel were on foot or on horseback. Apart from tracks the only roads were those left by the Romans. Both were in bad repair, and often infested with thieves and vagabonds. It is stated in an account of the Battle of Flodden (1513) that, in marching from York to Newcastle the roads were so bad that one of the guides leading the Earl of Surrey's army was almost drowned in a pot hole. Much of England was covered with forest, and such travel as took place was very slow. It is far easier now to travel from England to Australia than it was then to journey from London to York.

The man in the fields, ancestor of our old friend the man in the street, rarely, if ever, saw any actual money. He was paid for his work either in kind or by being allowed to cultivate his small strip of land alongside the land of his master. Money, of course, was still needed, since the King's taxes had to be paid, and there was trade with Europe. In still earlier times money was needed to pay such things as the Danegeld. This led to large quantities of English Pennies going to what is now Scandinavia, and there being copied, but this is another story.

So, for these and many other reasons money was made

locally under the overall direction of the king, in some cases his bishops and the gold—and silversmiths. At one time, around the Norman Conquest (1066), some 100 towns were making their own coins. What is more interesting still is the fact that these early Pennies, the only coin in use at that time and for many years to come, have on them not only the name of the town in which they were struck but the name of the man who struck them.

So much of interest has been turned up by the small amount of digging so far carried out that the beginner can see something of the large field that remains to be explored. Something more will be said later about the coinage of Britain and of other countries. A point has been reached when something should be said about how coins may be collected.

CHAPTER THREE

How to Collect

Taken at its simplest level, how to collect coins and medals can be summed up in the phrase, with judgment and care. Obviously judgment will be acquired fairly rapidly with the experience of building up the collection. The collector soon begins to see how to judge a good and desirable coin, bearing in mind the theme or pattern of the collection he is building. In giving some hints on the second requisite, care, judgment will be seen to be growing up in the background.

Care: primarily for the condition of a coin. Such condition is usually more important than the rarity of the coin. However common a coin may be its condition is of the greatest importance. Any collection of coins that is reasonably complete along the lines of the collecting pattern chosen by the collector must contain both its rare and its common pieces. The more common a piece may be, the more important is its condition. A rare coin may have to be accepted in poorer condition, since nothing better may be available. Among the more common coins the collector can afford to pick and choose and to take his time over obtaining a choice specimen.

To grade the relative condition of coins a number of recognised symbols are used among collectors. A coin in first class condition is usually described as Fleur-de-coin. This is abbreviated to F.D.C. It is a condition usually associated with ancient, hand-struck coins that have not only been perfectly produced, so far as methods allowed, but have been well preserved and have toned and mellowed with time.

In more recent times the terms Uncirculated, Mint State,

Brilliant Uncirculated, and others similar have come to be accepted as of almost equal value, particularly when applied to more modern coins. Over this equation there can be some differences of opinion. Uncirculated means just that, but the word is almost as elastic as the term second-hand in other fields. Second-hand has come to mean no more than not new.

Unless a coin is obtained direct from the mint it is obviously not new. It may have passed from one collection to another and thus never have circulated. It can still, therefore, be in mint state. Even so, as will be seen in a moment, modern minting methods provide practically every coin struck with some blemishes. With modern coins these blemishes have to be accepted in moderation when considering a coin that is uncirculated or in mint state.

To obtain an Ancient coin F.D.C. would seem to be almost an impossibility. But the chances, particularly in the Greek and Roman series, of coins being in this condition are greater than might be imagined. This is partly due to the fact that such coins never circulated in the manner of modern coins. As has been stated in referring to the early English Pennies, the free circulation of coins as we know it today, when practically nothing can be done without the passing of coins from hand to hand is, numismatically speaking, a fairly modern development. Why this is so is partly a matter of social history, too long to be detailed here. The result is that some very old coins in most series can be obtained F.D.C. though the condition is not common.

From the time when coins came into the hands of everybody as a necessary means of livelihood, mint state took on a slightly broader aspect. With the greater need for coins came mechanical methods of production. Where once coins were struck singly, by hand in the way we have seen, machines of ever increasing speed were now evolved to produce coins in ever increasing quantities. A brief explanation can, therefore, be given at this point on the development of machine produced coins.

The very early mechanical methods of coin production did not differ so very much from the hammered process. Broadly, the first step was the employment of wind, horse and water mills to drive rollers, which were used to reduce the bars of metal from which coins are produced to an even thickness. They were the ancestors of the domestic mangle and the huge rolling mills in the steel works of the world. Hence the word 'milled' became applied to coinage: from the source of power supply. Over the centuries a confusion has arisen on the use of this word. A coin does not have a milled edge. The vertical lines on the edge of a coin are properly known as graining.

Once the metal was rolled by the mill to an even thickness, the blanks or flans were punched out, like cutting out circles of dough when baking jam tarts. For some time these blanks were still fed into the coining press by hand, and the press was operated by men turning it by hand. The principle was the same as the old-fashioned letter-copying press, though the coin press was much bigger and heavier, and was often actuated very swiftly by men, running round in a circle drawing after them leather straps attached to the handle of the press, the speed of the men and the weight of the press producing a heavy blow. The blanks being fed in, and the coins taken out by hand, it was not uncommon for the operative to lose a finger or two if he were not quick enough, especially when primitive mechanical power began to be put to the work of driving the press as well as the rollers.

It was Boulton and Watt who adapted steam power to the driving of the whole machinery of a mint. Matthew Boulton (1728–1809) was a Birmingham manufacturer who, inheriting a business from his father, gradually increased its scope till he became the originator of modern mass production. In so doing he also laid the foundation of what has now become known as the time and motion study: both these in a small way. He took into partnership James Watt (1736–1819) who had been working, among other things, on the improvement of the primitive steam engine. As a reasonably satisfactory engine evolved these two men looked around for any and every purpose to which it could be put. While it was left to others to make the steam engine run on the road or on rails, Boulton and Watt applied its stationary power to a large number of useful purposes, ultimately to driving mint machinery.

Soon the new power-driven machinery was turning out coins at a speed which no hand could catch. The coins were, therefore, expelled from the presses, and fell into a container, usually nothing better than a tin bowl. Thus they damaged themselves as they struck together. Examination of a coin fresh from the mint will show some of the bruises and blemishes so produced. So, mint state when applied to a modern coin must accept a reasonable number of such blemishes in currency pieces. For proof and pattern pieces, of which more in its place, the presses are slowed down, even to striking coins singly, and each coin is very carefully treated at all stages of its production.

Below Mint State, Uncirculated and similar designations of new condition, the next state of a coin is described as Extremely Fine, abbreviated to E.F. Such a coin may have had a very limited wear before it reaches the hands of the collector. With modern coins it may have come straight from the mint. but have some of those blemishes referred to above.

Next down the scale is Very Fine, abbreviated to V.F. A coin in this condition is worth adding to a collection if a better specimen is not available, save perhaps at a very high price. Alternatively, it may be accepted as a gap-filler till a better specimen becomes available. As an exchange piece it will probably not realise as much as it originally cost.

Below V.F. come Fair or Fine, abbreviated to F. M. for Mediocre and P for Poor Condition.

As one goes down the scale the question of rarity enters more into consideration. If a coin is so rare that it cannot be obtained in mint state, or extremely fine, it may become acceptable to the collector in the lower levels of condition, since no better condition can be obtained. Even so the keen collector will always look around for a similar coin in slightly better condition.

Thus, rarity has begun to enter the picture. Rarity can, of course, stand on its own, or be allied to condition in the manner outlined above.

Rarity is often indicated by an accumulation of R's. RRRR is used to indicate a coin of the highest rarity, RRR to indicate extremely rare, RR to indicate very rare, R for rare and S for scarce. There is not much below this in the rarity scale, though C, where used, means common.

This system of multiple R's is elastic enough to meet almost any contingency, but it is hardly precise enough to meet modern issue conditions. Some rethinking on the subject of rarity therefore became necessary as modern issues increased in interest among collectors. The following system was, therefore, devised:

R7	only one or two examples known
R6	three or four examples known
R5	five to ten examples known
R4	eleven to twenty examples known
R3	extremely rare
R2	very rare
R	rare
S	scarce
N	normal, neither scarce nor common
C	common
C2	very common
C3	extremely common

Obviously the lower categories are not often used, but they are a helpful guide when the range as a whole is strictly applied. In dealing with modern issues the higher degrees of rarity are quite often only applicable to pattern and proof pieces. The above scale was evolved from one long in use in Europe.

From 1870, when Mint Reports were first published by the Royal Mint in London, exact figures for British and Commonwealth and for many foreign coins struck in London became available. It is, therefore, possible after this date to relate the above scale of rarity values to actual quantity figures. Many of the standard catalogues of modern coins of various countries referred to in the bibliography publish such figures.

There is still another rarity scale devised by the author of *English Copper, Tin and Bronze Coins in the British Museum*, the standard official catalogue on the coins of this series. The author states, 'to gauge and suitably to indicate the relative rarity of a large series of coins is always a troublesome business, especially when, as in this instance, coins upwards of 350 years old, and often of considerable rarity, have to be listed on a scale at the other end of which are the latest issues in circulation'. After considerable thought on this problem the author, making basic use of an existing rarity scale, extended it to the following:

EXC	excessively common
EC	extremely common
VC	very common
C	common
S	scarce
VS	very scarce
R	rare
VR	very rare
ER	extremely rare
EXR	excessively rare
PU	probably unique

In passing it may be said the unique, used as a rarity value for a modern coin, is one of the most dangerous of descriptions. It is almost unheard of for one single specimen only to be struck in a series of modern coins. If a modern coin is offered to a collector as an unique piece, its history and the class to which it belongs should be investigated with the greatest care. When it is remembered that to produce a modern coin, artists and engravers have to be paid, dies cut and hardened, mint operatives and production power paid for, then the chances of only one coin resulting, even a pattern or proof, are extremely unlikely.

The last two systems of rarity listed above prove very flexible in use; particularly is this so with the modern type of coin, where production figures are often in millions. It has to be remembered that the more millions of coins that are produced, the more they are likely to circulate since there must be a great demand for them. The more desirable it then becomes to find a really good specimen for the collector's cabinet. On the other hand, the greater the number of coins produced and the more wear they have, the more expendable they become; that is, the more they are called in and melted down, their metal content being used again. Paying in worn coin for melting down is one of the duties undertaken by the banks. It is not usual to see a British coin in circulation that has become very badly worn. The use of large numbers of badly worn coins is another invitation to the forger.

Having said something of what to look for in coins themselves, a few words can be added on the sources of supply. Broadly these can be divided into four basic categories. They are, coin dealers, auction sales, purchases from general antique dealers and other sources, and purchases or exchanges among friends, and at coin club meetings.

In Britain there are three main coin dealers whose names are household words among collectors throughout the world. They employ and train staffs who are, or who become, experts on numismatics and all its ramifications. Frequently individual members of such staffs specialise in the coins of one or more series; taken as a whole, they can deal with the coins of the world in any series and of any period. Such firms as these have considerable prestige and reputation to maintain, so that they can be absolutely trusted for their advice whether buying or selling coins. Two of the three issue monthly magazines and coin lists. These contain articles of interest to collectors and lists of coins offered for sale, as well as information on new issues and general coin-dealing news. As considerable stocks of coins, medals, reference books, and numismatic supplies are normally carried, these magazine-lists build up, over a period of years, into quite reasonable coin catalogues. Over a similar period they also indicate market trends and the popularity of the various series available.

With the increasingly lively state of the coin collecting market the number of dealers increases steadily. Some of these have been established for a considerable number of years, while others have only recently come into this particularly specialised form of business. The majority are honest and hard working, with their own reputations to maintain. Many of them do not attempt to cover the whole series of world coins, but specialise along various lines. This can be of advantage to the coin collector.

In Europe and America the picture is much the same; a small number of internationally known dealers and a large number of smaller dealers, often concentrating on a smaller or more specialised field of coin dealing.

Any coin dealer throughout the world who is a member of the International Association of Professional Numismatists can be trusted absolutely. This Association has been formed by the leading dealers for the protection of both the collector and the dealer, and for the dissemination of trade and professional knowledge and advice. Dealers can be, and are, barred or expelled from the Association for malpractices; equally, the names of fraudulent customers are circulated, and a general eye is kept on the whole scene of dealing and collecting, for the protection of all concerned.

In assessing dealers the date of their foundation and the fact that they have established premises where their business is conducted in public should weigh in their favour, as also should the fact that they work at coin dealing full time. On the other hand many part-time dealers have become firmly established through honesty and hard work, and have later become established full-time dealers. The beginner should bear in mind that there are black sheep in any gathering, so that it is hardly necessary to suggest that he is well advised to place his trust in an established dealer who has a reputation to protect. This is no more than common practice in any business.

In Britain one particular firm of auctioneers in London specialises in coin auctions, held at least once a month throughout the season. Two other famous auctioneering firms have occasional coin sales. Through these three auction rooms pass the coin collections, both big and small, of almost the whole world. This is because, almost alone in Europe, the British Government is wise enough not to impose a tax on coins purchased at an auction sale, nor to raise a host of frustrating regulations against coins being imported into Britain for sale by auction. Abroad a collector may have to

13 A modern, uncirculated, machine-produced British Crown, 1965. The areas marked show places where the coin has sustained damage either before it left the Royal Mint or afterwards by being shaken up in a bag with many other pieces. It is still, strictly speaking, in mint state. **14** An Anglo-Saxon Sceatta, showing on the reverse, a charming little dragon. Dragons appear so frequently on coins that one could almost believe of some substance in the legend of their existence. (Coin in the British Museum). **15** The dodecagonal (12-sided) Threepence as it was first put into circulation in 1937. **16** A Maria Theresa Thaler. Though dated 1780, this piece was struck in the 1960's. **17** The Canadian Dollar of 1949, showing a ship. Struck to commemorate the Federation of Newfoundland with Canada in that year. The ship is the *Matthew* of John Cabot, so far as its appearance is now known. A Venetian merchant who settled in Bristol, Cabot set off in 1497 to discover the North-West Passage to India. Instead he discovered Newfoundland and the mainland of America, a year before Columbus discovered the West Indies. Such an event is worthy of commemoration on the most durable of all records, a coin. **18** A set of Irish coinage. The obverse, the harp, is common to all the denominations from Halfcrown to Farthing. All the reverses show local fauna

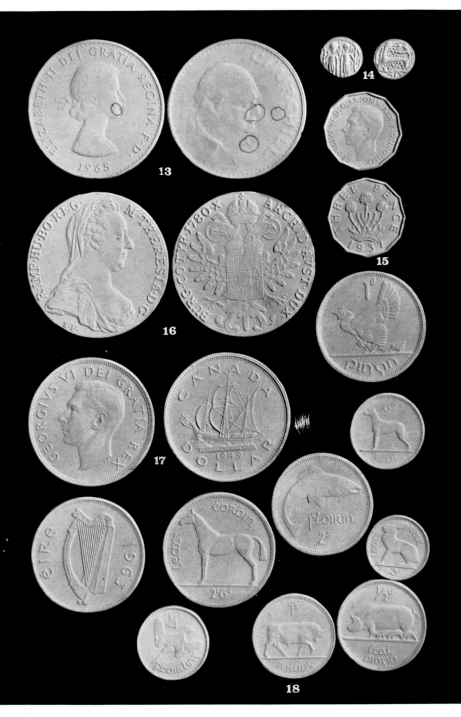

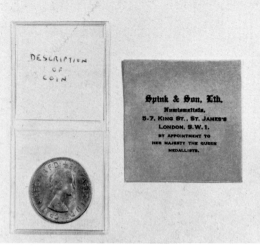

21 BELOW: The beautiful built-in coin cabinet by Chippendale, at Nostell Priory, Yorkshire. (Photo: courtesy H. S. Swann)

19 ABOVE: A 'double' transparent plastic envelope, in which both the coin and its description can be seen. A manilla envelope made from special dry paper, to hold a coin

20 BELOW: A 'knife box' with coins in ranked envelopes. An inexpensive but rather unsatisfactory method of keeping a coin collection. It is mainly useful for the collector who travels considerably and must either put his collection in a safe deposit or take it with him with a view to adding to it on his travels

pay as much as 25 per cent government tax on his purchase, which helps and encourages neither collector nor auctioneer.

As with the leading dealers, the leading auctioneers have reputations to maintain. They therefore spare no pains correctly to catalogue the coins in their sales. The compilation of such coin sale catalogues needs, like any other form of fine art dealing, considerable knowledge and experience of the subject. Such auctioneers offer the coins for inspection by the public some days before the sale, so that anyone who wishes can assess the value and interest to himself of any particular lots offered. Finally, such auctioneers are prepared to return to the seller, with a view to a refund to the purchaser, any coin which, in spite of all care, may prove to be false or to have been over-described as to condition. Alternatively they may take back such a coin and resell it later, more properly described. Obviously they can hardly be expected to do more.

It is not an infrequent occurrence for coins to form part of an auction sale in auction rooms outside London. With one or two notable exceptions, such sales are often held by property and general auctioneers. By reason of the diversity of their interests, many such auctioneers may lack specialised numismatic knowledge, and their catalogue descriptions can suffer accordingly. If a collector has sufficient knowledge there is sometimes the chance of picking up a bargain among poorly described coins. As more people collect, these chances become fewer.

The beginner should be warned, however, that even in the country he is liable to come into competition with the leading dealers in the sale room. It is part of the dealers function to keep all sales covered, not only in Britain but throughout the world. Since the larger dealers are well-known, the auctioneer has probably sent them a catalogue of the sale, being interested in getting the best price for himself and his client. Moreover, the dealer may not be there in person but may have placed his bids with a local representative, or with the auctioneer himself. It is always a little difficult bidding in the dark, 'against the book'.

From many points of view it is reasonable advice to a collector that when he starts to buy coins at the sales held by the international dealers and auctioneers, he should place his commissions with one of the dealers. The collector will only be charged a small percentage commission, calculated on the price realised, and for this commission he has the advantage of the dealer's knowledge, advice and service. The dealer may well have other customers' commissions already booked on any lots of interest or importance, as well as being interested in almost all the lots for his own stock purposes. To bid against dealers may, therefore, inadvertently prove a costly process. If a dealer knows that a collector is particularly interested in various items, he can advise the collector if his commission is not large enough, and may ask for some discretion in bidding where he feels that there will be keen competition over a lot. He will also advise if the collector's intended bid is wildly extravagent, and in any case will purchase the lot as far below the collector's commission as possible.

All this is established auction practice. Obviously a collector soon becomes suspicious if the lots on which he gives commissions are always purchased at the highest point, if he never seems to be successful in buying any lots, or if other things always seem to be going wrong. In actual fact the dealer is in a very vulnerable position and habitual sharp practice on his part will very soon be detected.

One small point should be made here, arising partly from the present great interest in coin collecting. There are some modern coins which appear fairly regularly in the sales and are liable to fetch an almost fixed price. Cased specimen sets might be a case in point. In such instances a bargain is unlikely, and the dealer may have to be given quite considerable discretion if the collector particularly wishes to obtain such a coin or coins.

The fact that a collector places his commission in the hands of a dealer does not prevent him from attending the auction sale in person if he so wishes, to watch over his interests and, if necessary, to join in the proceedings. Auction sales, it need hardly be said, can be quite exciting.

Since it may be felt that much of what has been said may tend to be too pro-dealer the author, himself an employee of the world's leading and oldest established numismatic dealers, can only say that such is his advice after some 30 years of dealing. Most people spend a limited amount of money on a hobby such as coin collecting, or allocate specific sums for use on this or any other form of investment. To go bull-headed into an auction room and bid against all comers in a specialised field such as that of coins is to court financial suicide. The larger dealers have no wish to prevent the individual buyer from bidding, or from buying his lot. Competition is healthy. But since the dealers must, by reason of the fact that they *are* dealers in a highly specialised field, hold most of the powerful cards in the game, to take them on single handed is risky.

It is easy to be carried away at an auction, once one's enthusiasm or antagonism is aroused. At least this can lead to a coin or coins being sold at far above their true value, thus establishing a false valuation. At worst it can dissipate the collector's money to bad advantage, and may eventually disgust him of his interest, perhaps under the idea that the dealers are a ring. Rings at auction sales are illegal in Britain anyway. The established dealer will always look after your interests. You are his bread and butter.

Casual purchases from ordinary antique dealers can be fun. You may singe a finger or two at first but there is always the chance of picking up a bargain, or a much desired piece. A good many years ago the average antique dealer knew little about coins. In these days of the popular reference book he not often knows quite a lot about coins, but actually stocks them on purpose. This makes the searching and bargaining all the keener, but the chances of purchasing a rare piece at little cost are the fewer. It is always worth while seeing what can be found, especially when visiting a strange town, perhaps on a holiday tour.

Purchasing and exchanging at coin club meetings is an excellent way of disposing profitably of unwanted coins. The purchase of an interesting miscellaneous lot of coins will always give the collector some pieces he does not want. There is always someone else who does want them, and the club is an excellent exchange ground. Most coin clubs hold a small annual auction, partly for the benefit of club funds. The event is usually one of the happy evenings in the club calendar. More will be said about clubs in a moment.

Reference has been made here and there to the price of experience. This does not mean that false coins are met with on every hand and forgeries at every turn. Generally speaking forged coins are mainly found among the more expensive and rare pieces. They were made purposely to deceive the collector, and professional advice is always needed when dealing with rarities, especially among coins in the Classical series.

But experience can be slightly costly in other ways. Miscellaneous buying of anything and everything can dissipate quite a lot of money. This is one reason why specialisation is of importance. It is realised that quite a lot of collectors have no set idea of any specialised line of collecting for perhaps some years. They may also start off on a new interest and wish to discard an interest already being followed. But unless a collector plunges wildly into collecting he can usually dispose of coins he no longer wants, quite often to advantage. Here again the dealer can often help since, if the collector takes that part of the collection of which he wishes to dispose and offers it to the dealer, at the same time buying from the dealer coins in his new field of interest, he will normally be generously treated. The dealer will make a profit out of the new interest, and is often willing to accept only a small profit on the coins he buys from the collector.

Like any other form of investment, only normal business acumen is needed by the collector. This and knowledge will grow together.

CHAPTER FOUR

Housing a Coin Collection

So far a few notes have been given on coin collecting and some of the pleasures which it holds. It has probably occurred to the beginner that, in building up a coin collection, some consideration has to be given as to how the collection is to be housed.

It can be said at once that nothing can be worse from the point of view of the coin itself than to keep it loose in a box, knocking against its fellows. It has already been shown what happens to coins at the mint when they fall together. If a coin is worth acquiring, it is worth looking after. It is wise, therefore, to consider at an early stage how coins can be properly housed.

The simplest method of keeping a coin safely and protecting it from damage is to place it in a small coin envelope. These are normally about 2½ inches square and are now available in two types, manilla and transparent plastic. Envelopes of about this size will take the majority of coins, up to crown or silver dollar size.

The manilla envelopes are specially made from very dry paper. Envelopes made from paper containing a high percentage of water will cause a silver coin to turn black. The plastic envelopes are inert, and should cause no damage. It is emphasised that in both cases such envelopes are made for the purpose of holding coins, so some thought has been given to the material used.

Each type of envelope has its advantages. On the paper envelope the collector can write the details of the coin which it contains, but he cannot see the coin. With the plastic envelope the coin can be seen, but nothing can be written on the envelope by normal means, dealing with the coin. Recently, to overcome this objection somewhat, a double pocket plastic envelope has been devised, one pocket taking the coin and the other a descriptive label. One advantage of the plastic envelope is that if the collector joins a coin club, it is possible to exhibit a coin in its envelope and for it to be passed round among club members without the coin itself being touched. This may seem to be taking protection to extreme length, but damp hands can damage the surface of a coin. The most careful of collectors may sometimes drop a coin on the floor, which may not improve it. Coins should not be dropped on hard surfaces, not rubbed with damp or dirty hands.

For storage purposes the envelopes can be ranked in long narrow cardboard boxes, sometimes known as knife boxes. While this is in many ways adequate, it has some obvious disadvantages. Only with trouble can any particular coin be found when required. Only with some effort can coins be kept in some particular order. On the other hand, a collection so housed is easily portable. In these days when more collectors travel greater distances to attend coin club meetings, or even greater distances to speak to or visit other clubs, a section of a collection carried in envelopes in a knife box easily slips into the overnight bag, is light enough to be carried by those who travel by air to visit clubs abroad: again an increasing number: and is constantly under the eye of the owner.

After the individual coin envelope, the next step is the coin album. In Europe such albums have only recently gained acceptance, but in America various types of albums have been developing for a decade or two.

The type of coin album recently developed in Britain consists of a variation of the ring binder. The binder used is specially made for the particular purpose and is covered with an attractive plastic, resembling leather. Transparent plastic pages, consisting in effect of a number of coin pockets joined together, are inserted on the rings. The pockets are available in two sizes, respectively large enough to take coins of crown or half-crown size. These two sizes are adequate for a general collection unless the collector is specialising in very large or very small coins.

In view of the weight which each page will have to support when all the pockets which it contains are filled with coins, care has been taken to see that the ring-holes are strongly made so that they do not tear away from the rings in normal use. White interleave pages for insertion between the plastic pages are available. These serve two purposes; that of making a good background for the coins in the various pockets, and that of displaying written descriptions of the coins themselves. Such coin albums can be kept in a bookcase, along with the various reference books which the collector will need as his collection grows.

Just as the well-known ring binder has been adapted into a book-form coin holder, so has the box file. For the purpose of coin storage the file has been fitted with some half-dozen coin trays, made of fibreboard. Such board is specially dried, and so is not likely to affect the coins.

The coin trays which are fitted into the box file are pierced with a number of circular holes, various sizes being available. One tray may have holes big enough to take crowns, another shillings, and so forth. Since the underside of each tray is flat and smooth, when the trays are fitted into the box file container they fill it completely. When the file is stood on end in a bookcase the coins in their various holes will not fall out.

While it has been suggested that in the case of the coin album the details of each coin can be written on the white interleaves, in the case of the box file method of storage this cannot be done. For the box file, as for the traditional coin cabinet, of which more in a moment, circular tickets of thin card are available from most coin dealers. Such circular tickets can be placed under each coin, and on them can be written the details of the coin, its date of purchase, the price paid for it, and any amount of other detail desired by the collector. Here again, such coin tickets, as they are usually called, are made from thin dry card and will not affect the coin which reposes on them. Apart from all else, the details written on such coin tickets will help to ensure that when coins are taken out of their respective places they can easily be returned.

It was stated a moment ago that one of the details that can be written on the coin ticket is the price paid for the coin to which the ticket refers. Most collectors like to remember what they paid for each coin and, quite naturally, like to keep such information private. To this end many collectors make use of some simple code. Such a cost code is easily devised by the use of a word of ten letters in which no one letter is repeated. A name such as Fishbourne: the name of a town: gives from left to right the figures 1 to 9, followed by 0. Thus, a coin which cost the collector £2 5s. 0d. codes as I/B/E, and so forth. It is wise to know what was paid for any particular coin, if only for the purposes of insurance. It is also of interest to the collector to note any appreciation in the value of any coin or coins over the years.

The above observations have drifted a little away from the actual subject of housing a coin collection, though they are germane to it. The box file method of keeping coins, last referred to, is perhaps an intermediate step between the coin album and the coin cabinet.

For several centuries the traditional method of keeping a coin collection has been in a coin cabinet, made of specially selected wood, usually mahogany or rosewood. Such wooden coin cabinets began to be made in about the eighteenth century. To quote from a recent article on the subject by H. S. Swann, ('Coin and Medal Cabinets' in *Coins and Medals*, vol. 1, No. 3, January–March 1965, p. 121), 'cabinet makers in the eighteenth century were quite often employed in producing special fitments for country mansions, to house the owner's collection of coins and medals. One such cabinet, which can with certainty be attributed to Thomas Chippendale, is still at Nostell Priory near Wakefield.

'One of the finest of the Georgian cabinet makers was William Vile, whose medal cabinet, made for George III, is well known. In more recent times, cabinets made by Turton, a Victorian furniture manufacturer, are good examples of craftsmanship'.

As stated above, such coin cabinets are usually made of well seasoned mahogany or rosewood, since it is important that the wood should be dry and free from natural oils or acids, both of which will damage a coin.

Over the centuries coin cabinets have been made in sizes from about a 9-inch cube to that of a cupboard. Essentially they consist of a carcase into which a number of thin shallow trays are fitted. Each tray is tongued on two opposite edges, the tongues sliding into horizontal grooves which are built into the sides of the main carcase.

The trays themselves are pierced with circular holes, each intended to contain one coin. The base of each hole contains a smaller hole so that the coin can be pushed up from below by the finger when it has to be removed from its place. This prevents damage to the edge of the coin if it should be a tight fit. Coins should never be dug out of a tray with a finger nail or the pointed blade of a penknife. Either method of extraction can damage the edge of the coin, and thus lower its value.

To give an example of such damage would be worth digressing for a moment. In 1937 the Royal Mint struck a number of proof sets of coins showing the designs to be used for the coinage of the reign of George VI, who was crowned in that year. The four gold coins, £5, £2, £1 and £½, were put into a small fitted leather case in which each reposed in a velvet lined hole. For some reason the Five-pound piece fitted very tightly into its individual position and could not be lifted out freely. In order to free it many people seem to have inserted the pointed end of a penknife blade. This left a cut on the smooth polished edge of the coin. When this set of now very valuable coins is offered to a dealer, one of the first things he does is to remove the Five-pound piece to see if it has been so cut on its edge. If it has, the value of the whole set is lowered. The collector cannot take too much care of his more valuable coins.

To return to coin cabinets: most have one or two doors, which can be securely locked. The smaller size of coin cabinet is easily portable and is often fitted with handles at the sides. A whole collection of valuable coins can, therefore, be conveniently removed in its cabinet to a safe, should the owner so wish. This is a point worthy of consideration by the owner of a collection who is, perhaps, going away from his place of residence for some considerable time. Valuable coins once stolen are not so easily replaced. As with other valuables, the insurance money will not replace some lost treasure.

Not many really large coin cabinets still exist, or are asked for. Such cabinets presuppose a collection of great size, and must be a safe deposit in themselves since they cannot be easily moved. For the collector of today the more popular sizes of coin cabinet range up to about 20 by 12 by 10 inches. Such cabinets can contain some 16 to 18 trays which, according to the size of the piercings, can house a total of over 1,000 coins.

Until quite recently such cabinets were only obtainable at second hand. This was partly because suitable, well-seasoned, wood of the required type was scarce, because the market for such cabinets was small, and because much of the manufacture of such cabinets must be done by hand. In the present age of mass production there remained few craftsmen who could undertake such specialised cabinet making.

Recently, however, a master cabinet maker took the problem in hand, solved the question of providing suitable wood, and evolved a series of basic cabinet sizes with interchangeable trays, and was thus able to put on the market a custom-built range of coin cabinets at reasonable prices. According to size, capacity, and finish, prices range from about £20 upwards.

It might be suggested that coin cabinets could be made from modern man-made plastic materials, some of which are available in excellent imitations of the finer woods. Some experiments have been made along such lines, but since the plastics industry thrives mainly on repetition work and the market for coin cabinets is small, the result of such experiments were not an economic proposition. Experiments have also been made with metal coin cabinets. Here again they proved expensive to produce for a small market, as well as having certain other disadvantages.

Experience tends to show that there is nothing much better than a mahogany or rosewood coin cabinet, of whatever size. In itself it is a nice piece of furniture, which polishes and tones with time, is generally no bigger than the average television set, and is an object of which the collector can be proud. In it his collection will rest secure under the best possible conditions. Each coin has its own place, with its disc of felt and its coin ticket beneath it. The trays can be removed from the cabinet, and the coins can be handled and studied at any time.

But even in the coin cabinet there can be small disadvantages. In buying such a cabinet one important factor at least has to be borne in mind. This concerns the selection of the various sizes of piercings in the trays: the sizes of the holes into which the coins will be put. If a tray is pierced to take 40 crown size coins it can only be used to its full advantage if 40 such pieces are placed in it. Small coins in large piercings waste costly space. If the tray is pierced to take 80 shilling size coins, no larger coin than a shilling can be placed in it.

Coins must, therefore, be kept according to size. This does not meet the requirements of all collectors, in particular those who like to keep relatively modern coins in sets of denominations, such as a date set of coins from Crown to Threepence.

Again, if a collector has a range of dates of shillings, arranged in date order in an 80 coin tray, and an intermediate date is added to the collection, perhaps some 70 coins may have to be moved in order to accommodate the new piece in its correct position in the sequence of dates. This does not become a really serious matter until a tray is completely filled. Then several trays or even the whole contents of the cabinet may have to be rearranged, and the collector may find himself faced with keeping Sixpences in Crown size piercings. He may even find that he has no large size piercings left vacant, and so have a Crown or two that will not go into his cabinet.

A partial solution to this problem is to have one or more plain drawers, about as thick as two coin trays, made to fit into the cabinet below the coin trays themselves. Sets of coins are sometimes purchased in fitted cases. Modern coins are frequently offered in plastic containers. These have to be housed somewhere if the sets are not to be broken up. The drawer is an obvious answer. It will take the odd very large coin or commemorative medal, and can hold the odd piece left out of some arrangements in the trays above.

Another solution to the problem is to have a cabinet entirely fitted with shallow drawers, and a supply of small shallow cardboard boxes made to fit into these trays. Such boxes have to be related in size so that, say 12, 24, 48 and so forth, will fit into the same tray area. These related boxes can then be moved around within the tray area to almost any extent. Both the boxes and the cabinet will have to be made to order, and can thus be rather costly. Most collectors would rather spend the money on coins, and put up with such shortcomings as the average coin cabinet may have.

Such an idea does, however, have some appeal to the commemorative medal collector. Commemorative medals, about which something will be said in its place, are almost always larger and thicker than coins. The medal collector therefore has little option than that of keeping his collection in open trays, with or without boxes, such as those mentioned above. In the latter case thin strips of wood, placed longitudinally across each tray, will retain the medals in reasonably ordered ranks.

Collectors of war medals and decorations, about which also something will be said later, have their own storage problems. They have not only to contend with the medals themselves, but with the ribands, neck collars, breast stars, and so forth. For these collectors the plain open tray is probably the only answer though, if money is available, obviously anything can be done to order.

CHAPTER FIVE

Numismatic Societies and Clubs

At this point in the story of coin and medal collecting it might be well to set down some details concerning numismatic societies and clubs. Such advice as has been offered may have helped the potential collector, but still may have left him with the feeling that he is 'going it alone'.

This is not so in fact. Coin clubs and societies have been mentioned. Their purpose is obvious from their title, that of drawing together coin collectors so that they can enjoy the company of others of like interest. There is probably no better advice that can be offered to the beginner in the coin collecting field than that of joining a coin club so soon as he feels the urge to collect. At his local coin club, however ignorant he may feel on the subject of collecting, he will be among others who have travelled the same road as he himself. He will be surrounded by fellow members who welcome him, understand the problems of the beginner, and who will readily advise him and help in any way they can.

Having visited many of the coin clubs and societies in Britain, the author can say, without fear of contradiction, that the atmosphere among members is one of geniality and encouragement, that new members are most welcome, and that all will be done that can be done to make them feel at home. A few words about coin clubs and the work that they have done in the interests of coin and medal collectors will not, therefore, be out of place.

In the last 20 or 30 years the growing interest in coin and medal collecting has brought into being coin clubs and societies in all parts of Britain. From them has sprung the

63

British Association of Numismatic Societies, and to this Association most of the clubs and societies are affiliated. The Association, therefore, speaks with one voice in matters which we shall consider in a moment.

Of first importance is the Association's Year Book. From this publication are listed the various affiliated societies and their places of meeting.

ANGLO-AMERICAN COIN CLUB. Founded 1965. Meetings at A.Y.A. Building, R.A.F., West Ruislip, at 7.30 p.m. on the second and fourth Mondays of each month.

BATH AND BRISTOL NUMISMATIC SOCIETY. Founded 1950. Meetings: (1) at the City of Bath Technical College, Lower Borough Walls, Bath, at 7.30 p.m. on Friday, monthly from October to May; (2) at the City Museum or the University, Bristol, at 7.15 p.m. on Thursdays, monthly from October to May.

BIRMINGHAM NUMISMATIC SOCIETY. Founded 1964. Meetings at various places in Birmingham on alternate Wednesdays, beginning at 7.30 p.m.

BUCKINGHAMSHIRE NUMISMATIC SOCIETY. Founded 1961. Meetings at the Church Room, Whitchurch, Aylesbury, and at the Gravel Hill C.P. School, Chalfont St Peter, alternately on the first Wednesday of the month at 7.30 p.m.

CAMBRIDGESHIRE NUMISMATIC SOCIETY. Founded 1946. Meetings at the Friends' Meeting House, Jesus Lane, Cambridge, on the third Monday of the month from September to June, at 7.30 p.m.

CHELTENHAM NUMISMATIC SOCIETY. Founded 1953. Meetings held monthly (except August) alternately at 2.45 p.m. on the second Saturday at Cheltenham Museum, and at 7.45 p.m. on the second Friday at Members' houses.

COVENTRY AND DISTRICT NUMISMATIC SOCIETY. Founded 1954. Meetings at the Three Spires Hotel, Grayswood Avenue, Coventry, at 8 p.m. on the first Thursday of each month.

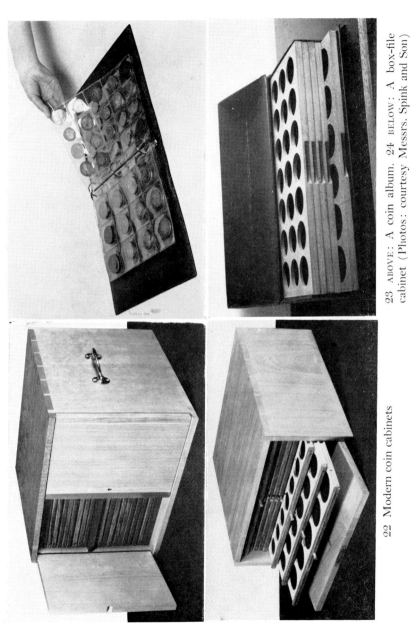

23 ABOVE: A coin album. 24 BELOW: A box-file cabinet (Photos: courtesy Messrs. Spink and Son)

22 Modern coin cabinets

DERBYSHIRE NUMISMATIC SOCIETY. Founded 1964. Meetings at the Genevieve Coffee House, Gower Street, Derby, on the second Monday of the month at 7.30 p.m.

HAYES (MIDDLESEX) AND DISTRICT COIN CLUB. Founded 1953. Meetings at the Yeading Lane Library, Hayes, Middlesex, at 8 p.m. on the third Thursday of each month.

HORNCASTLE AND DISTRICT COIN CLUB. Founded 1963. Meetings at The Black Swan Hotel, Horncastle, on the third Thursday of the month at 7.30 p.m.: at 7 p.m., December–February.

HUDDERSFIELD NUMISMATIC SOCIETY. Founded 1947. Meetings at the Tolson Memorial Museum, Ravensknowle Park, Huddersfield, at 7.30 p.m. on the first Monday of the month from September to June.

KENT NUMISMATIC SOCIETY. Founded 1913. Meetings at the Museum, Faith Street, Maidstone, on the second Friday of the month at 7 p.m.

LANCASHIRE NUMISMATIC SOCIETY. Founded 1864. Revived 1933. Meetings at the Central Hall, Oldham Street, Manchester, on the first Saturday of winter months at 2.30 p.m. and on the first Wednesday of summer months at 6.15 p.m.

---

25 The 50 Lepta of modern Greece. A cupro-nickel piece, the obverse design looks back to great days of coin artistry in Ancient Greece. The sardonic smile on the face of a one-time Greek Goddess seems to ask: to what base uses are we descended? **26** The gold 10 Francs of the now tourist state of Liechtenstein, one of the sole remaining states of those into which much of Europe was once divided. **27** The aluminium-bronze 2 Franc piece of the 'golden' state of Monaco. **28** The silver Rouble struck to commemorate the 300th anniversary of the Romanoff Regime in Russia, a regime so soon afterwards to be swept from all but the pages of history. **29** The bronze One Cent piece of Sarawak, symbolic of the White Rajah, Malayan pirates and European 'progress' brought to the Far East. **30** One of the relatively few square coins issued for general circulation, the bronze One Cent piece of the then Straits Settlements, 1926. **31** The end of an Empire. The last type of Rupee, cupro-nickel, issued under British rule in India. It replaced a long series of silver Rupees, similar to number 32. **33** The first separate coinage of Southern Rhodesia is typified in the silver Half Crown of 1932

Lincolnshire Numismatic Society. Founded 1931. Meetings at 100 Hainton Avenue, Grimsby, on the third Wednesday of each month, at 7.30 p.m.

London Numismatic Club. Founded 1947. Meetings at the St Bride Institute, St Bride Lane, Fleet Street, City of London, E.C.4, at 6.30 p.m. monthly throughout the year.

Medway Towns Numismatic Society. Founded 1943. Meetings at Rochester Museum, Eastgate House, High Street, Rochester, at 7.30 p.m. on the first Friday of every month.

Merseyside Numismatic Society. Founded 1947. Meetings at the Common Hall, Hackins Hey, Dale Street, Liverpool 2, at 7 p.m. on the second Tuesday of each month from October to May, omitting December.

Numismatic Society of Nottinghamshire. Founded 1948. Meetings at the Albert Hall Institute, Derby Road, Nottingham, at 7.30 p.m. on the first Tuesday of each month from September to April.

Oxford Numismatic Society. Founded 1955. Meetings at the Ashmolean Museum and Oxford Union, Oxford, at 2.30 p.m. on Saturdays, monthly.

Reading Coin club. Founded 1964. Meetings at the Museum, Balgrave Street, Reading, at 8 p.m., rotating between Monday, Tuesday and Wednesday each month.

Rye Coin Club. Founded 1955. Meetings at the Library, Further Education Centre, Lion Street, Rye, at 7.30 p.m. on the second Thursday of each month.

St Albans and Hertfordshire Numismatic Society. Founded 1947. Meetings at the City Museum, Hatfield Road, St Albans, at 7.30 p.m. on the first Wednesday of each month, except August.

Scunthorpe & District Numismatic Society. Founded 1966. Meetings at Room 1, Highfield House Club, Shelford Street, Scunthorpe, at 7.30 p.m. on the last Thursday of each month.

SHEFFIELD AND DISTRICT NUMISMATIC SOCIETY. Founded 1946. Meetings at City Museum, Weston Park, Sheffield, at 7.30 p.m. on the third Wednesday of each month.

SOUTHAMPTON AND DISTRICT NUMISMATIC SOCIETY. Founded 1953. Meetings at the Bugle Hall, 53 Bugle Street, Southampton, at 7.30 p.m. on the second Friday of each month throughout the year.

SURREY NUMISMATIC SOCIETY. Founded 1961. Meetings at the 10th Croydon Scouts Headquarters, 115 St James' Road, West Croydon, at 7.45 p.m. on the fourth Wednesday of each month from September to May.

TYNESIDE NUMISMATIC SOCIETY. Founded 1954. Meetings at the Literary and Philosophical Society Library, Newcastle, at 6.30 p.m. on the first Wednesday of each month from October to May.

WESSEX NUMISMATIC SOCIETY. Founded 1948. Meetings at St Peter's Hall, Hinton Road, Bournemouth, at 7.30 p.m. on the first Friday of each month.

WEST MIDLAND NUMISMATIC SOCIETY. Founded 1960. Meetings at the Public Library, Dudley, at 7.30 p.m. on the second Wednesday of the month, excluding July and August.

YORKSHIRE NUMISMATIC SOCIETY. Founded 1909. Meetings at the Church Institute, Albion Place, Leeds, or at various Yorkshire towns as advertised, at 2.30 p.m. on the first Saturday monthly. No meetings are held in January, February and December.

Societies not yet affiliated

ABERDEEN COIN CLUB. Founded 1965. Meetings at the Trades Hall, Adelphi, Aberdeen, on the last Wednesday of each month.

GLASGOW & WEST OF SCOTLAND NUMISMATIC SOCIETY. Meetings at the British Legion Centre, Renfrew Street, Glasgow.

There are also other Societies not yet affiliated to the Association so that their details are not yet in the Year Book.

At the meetings of these societies a member, or perhaps a visiting speaker, usually gives a talk on a subject of interest. After this the meeting usually becomes open and conversation flows easily on topics of general interest.

Perhaps one or two suggestions might be offered on the subject of club membership. Unless you belong to the class of 'hermit' collector: one who hoards his collection to himself and gloats introspectively over his coins: you should join a coin club as soon as the interest grips you. Having done so, you should be prepared to pull your weight in due time, and so far as private commitments allow. Far too many coin clubs continue to exist because of the efforts, financial as well as administrative, of a few devoted members. Though many numismatic clubs have quite a small membership, they are growing fast now that coin collecting has spread to a far wider field than was possible only a few years ago.

As a member, therefore, you should be prepared to do your bit by serving on the committee for a spell, and by speaking at meetings on the subject of your own particular interest. This may take some courage, if you are of a retiring nature. But in speaking to your coin club members you are at least assured of a sympathetic audience. They are interested in what you have to say, and are willing to listen, to learn, and, of course, to criticise. So, jot down a few notes about what you have to say. If you still mistrust yourself, write the whole talk down and read it as a Paper. You will be respected for your time and trouble by your fellow members. In fact, herein lies something of a paradox. It would appear, from experience gained over many years of lecturing, that the more expert the speaker becomes, the more likely he is to present a carefully prepared Paper, rather than attempting to speak 'off the cuff'. The more you know about your subject, the more important it is to present it accurately.

The more you know about your subject, the more important it is to exclude extraneous matter, to be sure of your facts, so that you cannot be 'shot down' by the questions asked after the talk.

There is also another point, with which some may not agree. If you are speaking to your coin club, your listeners expect not only to be instructed, but to be entertained. Unless you happen to be a very facile speaker you may bore your audience, and never achieve either a theme or a point to your remarks.

Most coin clubs arrange their programme about a year in advance. If you are asked to speak, you therefore may have several months ahead of you in which to think over what you have to say, to do some small research into the background history of your subject, and to get it all down on paper, perhaps with some slides, photographs, and exhibits by way of illustration. In fact the background history behind the coins or medals about which you are speaking is as important as the coins or medals themselves. So, as you have probably some time in hand, get what you want to say down on paper, embellish it with background history and, if possible, by some slides for projection and some examples of the coins or medals about which you are speaking. You can then go to the meeting at which you are to speak with a feeling of security about what you are going to say. Nothing has been left to chance.

Finally, say what you have to say slowly. This not only impresses your audience but gives them time to assimilate what you are talking about and the various points which you wish to put over. Speaking at high speed on a technical subject only gives your audience mental indigestion, bores them, and makes them give up the attempt to follow your various technical points.

Stress was laid, a few moments ago, on the importance of doing your bit as a club member. Some genius in Canada recently wrote down how *not* to act as a club member. Since his comments are only too true they are worth repeating here; and of thinking over.

Ten ways to wreck a Coin Club

1. Do not go to the meetings.
2. When you do go, arrive late.
3. If the weather is bad, don't even think of going.
4. When you do attend a meeting, find fault with the President and other officers. (For President, read Chairman in English parlance.)
5. Never accept an office, after all it is much easier to sit back and criticise.
6. If you are appointed to a committee, don't attend its meetings but, if not, complain about it.
7. When your opinion is asked, reply that you have nothing to say. After the meeting, however, tell everyone how you would have handled the matter.
8. When others in the club are doing the lion's share, tell everyone that it is run by a clique.
9. Don't worry about paying your dues, wait till you receive two or three notices from the Secretary. That will keep him from running out of something to do.
10. Don't bother about getting new members. Let the ones who do all the work do that too.

A trifle bitter perhaps, but most club secretaries will endorse many of these points.

It has already been said that most of the clubs and societies in this country are affiliated to the British Association of Numismatic Societies. Many useful advantages flow from this affiliation. The most important of them is the annual National Numismatic Congress.

The National Congress is held through one particular local society, which acts as host for that particular year. The majority of the societies and clubs are small in membership as has been said. Financially they just about break even year by year. The prospect of organising the annual Congress may look like a financial impossibility. To meet this, the Association has a small bank balance from which limited funds may be drawn to help pay for the Congress. Additional to this, Congress Members pay a reasonable sum as Delegates, which money helps to defray the expenses of organisation of the Congress.

Time has shown that the Congress grows in strength year by year. It is usually held from a Friday evening till the following Sunday. Local municipal councils are becoming more aware of the standing of the Congress, and usually accord it a small Civic Reception.

On the Saturday the real business of the Congress is transacted. Speakers read Papers of general or local interest, interspersed with morning coffee, lunch, and a Congress dinner held in a local hotel in the evening. The Sunday session is usually devoted to organised trips to local places of interest, sometimes of numismatic importance, sometimes just local sight-seeing. Delegates are not pressed to join such trips; the choice is entirely their own. The whole Congress is happy and informal, and is the culminating event of the year for many British collectors. Delegates' wives and children are welcomed to the Congress, which is normally a most sociable event.

Another activity grows out of the Association. This is the annual Study Group, a meeting which is usually held in the spring of the year. For some years past it has often been held in Cambridge. Delegates usually stay the week-end in an hotel, and get down to some really interesting and instructive numismatic work. Here again the organisation is quite voluntary and a most useful session results. All collectors are welcome, as are offers of help in the general organisation. This annual Study Group is growing and should be better known.

From the local numismatic society and club, members can graduate (as it were) for membership of either or both of the two long-established numismatic societies, the Royal Numismatic Society, whose membership confers a Fellowship, and the British Numismatic Society, membership of which is equally respected. Members of both Societies undertake serious and important numismatic research. Medals are conferred for outstanding contributions to the science.

Both of these national Societies record their transactions in the *Numismatic Chronicle* and the *British Numismatic Journal*, respectively. Here the great names in numismatics, and often in history and archaeology, are to be found. As the beginner collector grows in stature there is nothing to bar his contribution to these transactions.

Most of the clubs and societies also record their transactions, and not a few of them publish their own annual journals. The activities of the local Societies as a whole are reported in the two privately owned periodicals, the *Numismatic Circular*, and the *Coin and Medal Bulletin*.

To sum up: membership of a club or society is to be strongly recommended. It adds much to the pleasures of collecting, stimulates research, and results in many firm friendships among collectors throughout the country. More than this: such clubs and societies exist throughout the world, and contacts between them are often close and frequent. Your own collecting interest is that of others, and numismatists throughout the world ask nothing better than contact with each other. Be prepared, therefore, to do your bit in helping your own society along. You are making your own small contribution to a world-wide picture. Such small contribution you will not regret.

CHAPTER SIX

Expanding the Collection

So far some advice has been offered on what to collect, how
to do so, on how to keep the collection, and how to enjoy it
through contact with others of a like interest at coin club and
society meetings. From this have stemmed a few notes on
British coinage, on the understanding that the beginner
will, quite naturally, take a primary interest in his own
coinage.

It has also been said that quite often a miscellaneous
handful of coins will fire the collecting interest. Such a
handful of coins must, of necessity, contain examples of the
coinages of various foreign countries. Because such coins are
not so easily understood and appreciated by the beginner,
the picture should now be expanded to take some account of
them. As an interlude between the consideration of more
serious matters a few coin stories follow; stories about coins
that could well be among those in the handful in question.

Some of the plates illustrate an apparently random
selection of coins, chosen to illustrate, with a few exceptions,
pieces struck since 1800. With coinage of this period most
of this account has so far been concerned. Since many
collectors start collecting along a simple line of interest, the
stories which follow are of a very general nature. At least
half the interest in coin collecting lies not in the coins
themselves but in the history that lies behind them. This
chapter may, therefore, be looked upon as a little light
entertainment. It has been said that the collector should, and
almost certainly will, specialise in some way as he progresses.

Some of the stories which follow may offer an idea or two on specialisation.

The piece that strikes us first, 16, is one of the exceptions to our dateline suggested above. It came originally from Austria. It is generally known as the Maria Theresa Thaler (Thaler = Dollar = Crown). Quite a story lies behind it.

Originally struck in Vienna, it attained over the years acceptance in parts of Africa, especially in Ethiopia. When it ceased to be a current Austrian coin there was still a strong demand for it from these territories. The local inhabitants, less educated than the Austrians, had come to know the piece in course of trade, and would accept no other.

As a result the piece continued to be struck, still dated 1780, new dies being provided as the old wore out. With the changing political aspect of Europe over the centuries the piece was at one time or another struck in Berlin, Paris, Rome, London, Bombay, and by The Mint, Birmingham Limited. Its official designation became now that of 'trade Dollar', under which title it began to be struck in Britain at the time when Mussolini invaded Abyssinia (= Ethiopia). During World War II it was again struck at the Royal Mint. Only a year or two ago was the striking passed back once more to Austria, where the piece continues to be struck.

Thus, though no longer currency in Austria, it is still in use as money in parts of Africa, for which it was never intended. So the Maria Theresa Thalers that were struck at all these various mints are not forgeries. They are legitimate later strikings to meet the demand for the piece in trade with countries where it alone would be accepted. Some similar story attaches to the British Sovereign.

Collectors of coins showing animals and birds are well served. The American Journal *The Numismatist* ran a feature page for some considerable time on the numismatic zoo. Animals are so numerous on coins that it is well to decide if purely heraldic representations are to be included in the collection. Animals are the commonest supporters of coats of arms. As stated previously, in ancient times animals were much used in coin design. One of the earliest of its breed is a funny little dragon on an Anglo-Saxon coin known as a Sceatta, a series of coins which date from the late seventh to the third quarter of the eighth century (14). As a mythical animal, he was later to become famous in conjunction with St George.

There are plenty of coins showing ships for those collectors with a maritime interest (17). The National Maritime Museum in Greenwich has what is probably the world's finest collection of coins and medals dealing with maritime matters, so a collector of such pieces is in good company. This fine collection is on view daily, and was largely assembled by the late Earl of Sandwich. The Dutch Naval Museum has a collection of equal interest. A word will be said later about the difficulties of displaying coins and medals to advantage. Much thought and ingenuity has been used in the presentation of the British Maritime Museum's collection.

Even so common a coin as our own little twelve-sided Threepence has an interesting story behind it (15). It was first designed, in a slightly different form, in anticipation of the new coinage to be issued in the reign of Edward VIII (1936). As Edward was never crowned, and a new British coinage cannot be issued till after the coronation, the new piece was not put into circulation during this short reign.

Since it was a coin of entirely new shape and weight a few unofficial specimens were struck for, it is said, the benefit of automatic coin-operated machines such as the public telephone and the railway ticket machine. A new British coinage has to be introduced by Royal Proclamation and when it was seen that there would be no coronation of Edward VIII the trial pieces were hastily rounded up. A few pieces escaped. They are of the greatest rarity, but can occasionally be seen in collections. They are dated 1937, in which year the coronation of Edward VIII would have taken place. They are very similar in design to the piece finally adopted, but the little plant on the reverse, the Thrift, received a slightly different artistic treatment. Meantime, to keep our coinage history accurate, a set of pattern pieces of the proposed coinage for the reign of Edward VIII was struck and is in the Royal Collection in Windsor Castle.

When the new coin, in the form illustrated, appeared in 1937 it was, it is said, scorned in Scotland, where the banks would have none of it. Owing to World War II it is only in comparatively recent years that the vending machines have been adapted to take the dodecagonal Threepence. The war itself helped to popularise the piece since it was instantly recognised by touch in conditions of blackout or poor lighting. It has continued to be issued in many millions, the design changing with the new coinage in 1953.

When British coins ceased to be struck in silver after 1946, the little silver Threepence disappeared, almost unlamented. It still survives as a denomination, struck in silver every year in small numbers for the Royal Maundy money, mentioned previously. In this series it still retains the large figure 3 on the reverse, a design that had been in use for some centuries prior to 1928. In that year the redesigned coinage of George V (1910–1936) was put into circulation, and the reverse design of the normally current threepence changed, leaving the reverse type with the figure 3 exclusively for the Maundy series. The figure 3 reverse type did not reappear on the normal Threepence in current circulation.   .

A point about recognising coins by touch: the new Australian decimal coinage put into circulation in 1966 is said, by the boldness of its reverse designs, to be easily recognisable by touch. This, it is hoped, will be helpful to blind people and those with failing eyesight.

When the then recently constituted Irish Free State issued its own coinage in 1928, nothing like it had ever appeared in the British Isles before (18). Gone were all the traditional heraldic symbols. In their place appeared on the various reverses local fauna. On the obverse appeared the Irish harp.

The reverse designs consisted of a horse, a salmon, a bull, an Irish wolfhound, a hare, a hen and chickens, a sow and litter, and a woodcock. These subjects were offered to eight artists for suitable treatment, bearing in mind that the designs submitted were for use on a coinage. The designs which the competitors submitted showed considerable individual treatment. Those of Percy Metcalf were accepted, with certain minor alterations. The new Irish coinage was struck at the Royal Mint, London, and has so continued. In the original 1928 issues the half crown, florin, and shilling were of silver, the sixpence and threepence in nickel, and the penny, halfpenny, and farthing in bronze. After 1951 all the silver coins were struck in nickel. The obverse design has passed through some minor changes, mainly as to the legend. A crown piece has just been struck; too late for inclusion here.

The 50 Lepta of Greece, 1930 (25) makes some attempt at imitating Ancient Greek coins, particularly on the obverse. The little gold coin number 26 is the 10 francs of the tiny State of Liechtenstein. With an area of only 62 square miles and a total population of some 13,500, this little State still survives from among the many princely states into which parts of Europe were once divided. Luxembourg, mainly known to us as a radio station, is another. Monaco is a third and its 2 franc piece (27) shows an archer, in this case Hercules.

The Russian piece (28) was struck to celebrate the 300th anniversary of the Romanoff regime in 1913. By 1917 this regime had been swept away by one of the greatest revolutions in modern history, leading to the establishment of the Union of Socialist Soviet Republics of Russia. One hears so much about the various leaders of this country that one is apt to forget that in fact Russia consists of a Confederation of Republics.

The Hungarian gold 100 Krona of 1907 is a coin that in its design resembles a commemorative medal. As a type it would be considered in many countries as too medallic to be wholly a coin. Its reverse shows the coronation scene which took place 40 years before. In Britain this type of reverse is reserved for such pieces as official coronation commemorative medals, of which something will be said later.

Coins commemorating some special event or the anniversary of such an event have a particular interest, and once again offer a line of specialisation along which a collection might be formed. There are a whole series of commemoratives in the coinage of the United States of America. They are a most interesting section of United States coinage, of which American collectors are justly proud. Of them R. S. Yeoman (*A Guide Book of United States Coins*), writes:

'Commemorative coins have been popular since the days of the Greeks and Romans. In the beginning they served to record and honor important events and in the absence of newspapers they proved highly useful in passing along news of the day.

'Many modern nations have issued commemorative coins and such pieces are highly esteemed by collectors. Yet no nation has surpassed our own country when it comes to commemorative coins and in this we have reason to be proud.

'The unique position occupied by commemoratives in United States coinage is largely due to the fact that with few exceptions they are the only coins that have a real historical significance. The progress and advance of people in the New World are presented in an interesting and instructive manner on the commemorative issues. Such a record of facts artistically presented on our gold and silver issues appeals strongly to the collector who favours the historical side of numismatics. It is the historical features of the commemoratives, in fact, which creates interest among many people who would otherwise have little interest in coins.'

Behind the bronze 1 Cent piece of Sarawak (29), lies a most unusual story. It is too long to be told in detail. Quite a number of books have been written on the subject, some factual, some more imaginary. Briefly, Sir James Brooke, seen on the coin, received the territory of Sarawak, part of the island of Borneo, in return for his help to the uncle of the Sultan, whom Brooke found engaged in a war with rebel tribes.

The title of Rajah and Governor of Sarawak was conferred on Brooke on 24th September, 1841. He set about his task as Rajah with a will, instituting free trade, framing a new code of laws, carrying out expeditions to stamp out piracy, always rabid among the islands of the Archipelago, and in general spared no effort to make a civilised country out of his territory.

Under his rule the population increased some 25 times and trade with Singapore boomed. The territory continued to be ruled by the Brooke family, becoming a British Protectorate in 1888, the Brooke family finally giving up the throne in 1946. During the rule of the Brooke family a range of silver and bronze coinage, from 50 to $\frac{1}{4}$ cent, was struck for the territory in Britain and put into general circulation. The heads of the three Rajahs appeared successively on the obverse, the last coin, a 1 cent piece, being struck in 1937.

There are not many square coins, but we see one, with suitably rounded corners, in the 1 Cent piece of the Straits Settlements (30). This section of the British Commonwealth coinage series is based on the Straits Settlements Dollar The coin, first issued as a silver piece in 1903, has not been struck since 1920. The second issue of silver Dollars was slightly reduced in size and the series as a whole was struck at the Royal Mint, the Bombay Mint, and with the H mint mark of Birmingham. Many such silver Dollars disappeared from circulation, to make dress ornaments for the native girls, while others, particularly those of 1919 and

1920, were used in native marriage ceremonies. Till recently these two latter years were considered scarce or rare pieces, though the Mint Reports showed that many had been struck. The present high price of silver has returned them to the bullion market in large numbers, mostly marked with the blue or red die smeared on them, it is said, as part of the ceremony referred to above. Coin number 31 is one of the last Rupees to be issued at the end of a numismatic story that started with the famous East India Company, saw the conquest of India, the 'Black Hole of Calcutta', the siege of Lucknow, and the title of Empress of India conferred on Queen Victoria. This immense page of history was some 200 years in the making.

The British administration imposed upon India as a whole an 'overall' coinage, based on the Rupee. The range contained silver, nickel alloy, and bronze pieces, some square, some with serrated or crenalated edges. The reverse ornamentation had a particularly oriental appearance, 32 often with the legends in several languages.

Apart from the 'overall' coinage, many of the States still titularly ruled by their own Sovereigns and government issued their own coinages. Some had the head or bust of the

34 The silver proof Crown of New Zealand, 1935. Known as the 'Waitangi Crown' by reason of the reverse design: Captain Hobson shaking hands with a Maori Chief: this first Crown piece marked the Jubilee of George V, not the centenary of the signing of the Treaty of Waitangi in 1840. This latter event was commemorated by a special Half Crown, struck in 1940. **35** Not as old as it looks. This 50 Mazuna piece of Morocco was not struck in A.D. 1289. **36** Another unusual shape for a coin issued for general circulation. A cupro-nickel Ten Cents of the Seychelles, 1939. Such a piece is usually described as having a serrated edge. **37** The first silver Dollar issued for circulation in Canada, 1935. Though such a Dollar had been designed in 1911, and is illustrated on another plate, this was the first issued for currency. Till then the Dollar was a 'paper name'. The 1935 Dollar marked the Jubilee of George V. **38** A group of four token coins, typical of a large series in use in Canada before a coinage was struck for the Dominion as one whole country. The first of the latter pieces are dated 1858–9

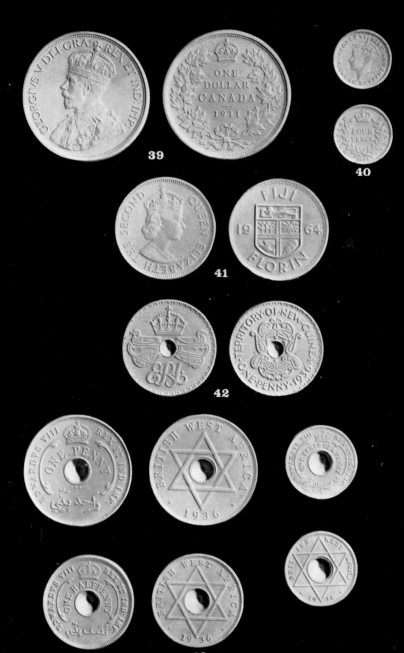

39

40

41

42

43

British Emperor or Empress, some that of the local ruling Prince. The coinage of the last hundred or so years of Indian history is, therefore, one full of interest and variety. It places before the collector as clearly as anything can the vast size and enormous population of India, its many states with their princely rulers, a few of whom it has been the author's great privilege to meet.

The lately controversial state of Southern Rhodesia had its first separate coinage under British rule in 1932, and the Half-crown is illustrated (33). Many of the Commonwealth territories throughout the world had coinages on the British model, with the Crown as the silver unit. In most cases no Crown was struck till some time after the inception of the local coinage. This holds good for Southern Rhodesia, whose first Crown appeared in 1953 to mark the coronation of Elizabeth II and the centenary of Cecil Rhodes, whose name the territory bears. It is an unusual piece in the British Commonwealth series in that it carries two portraits, that of the Queen and that of Cecil Rhodes. No coin has had two heads on it in the British and British Empire and Commonwealth series since the reign of William and Mary (1689–1694).

The same fact about the absence of a Crown till long after the establishment of a local coinage also holds good for

39 The coin that never appeared in circulation. A silver proof of the design for the Canadian Dollar of 1911, one of the rarest of the modern coins in the world, so far as is at present known. **40** The silver Four-pence or Groat, struck at the Royal Mint for use in far-away British Guiana. **41** The first British attempt at a decimal coinage, referred to earlier, was to have repercussions half a world away. The Florin, as used in the Fiji Islands. **42** The coinage of a king who never was crowned. The first piece to reach Europe was the bronze Penny of New Guinea. **43** It was closely followed by the cupro-nickel Penny, Half-penny and One Tenth Penny of British West Africa, and by the bronze Ten and Five cents of East Africa (not illustrated, but similar in appearance). It is said that the Tenth Penny is often used as a washer, since washers cost at least a halfpenny. In what places, then, will this little coin be found one hundred years from now?

Australia. Here the first Crown marked the coronation of George VI, 1937. Incidentally no half-crown have ever been issued in Australia, which had its first local coinage on the British model in 1910. A few words will be said about Australian coinage in a moment.

New Zealand had its first local coinage in 1933, but no Crown was struck till 1935, the piece then commemorating the jubilee of GeorgeV (34). With this Crown went a small numismatic mystery. Mint records show that Crowns were issued both as proof pieces (of which more later) and as pieces for circulation. In the event none of the latter has been seen, save for one or two pieces claimed as being observed by collectors. What happened to the currency pieces and where are they now?

The South African Crown issued under British rule only appeared in 1947, to mark the Royal Visit of George VI, though the local coinage on the British model was struck at Pretoria in and after the year 1923. In this particular case there had been a silver Crown struck locally before 1947. President Kruger issued such a piece from Pretoria as far back as 1892, for the South African Republic. It is said that the same coining presses were used to strike the 1947 Crowns.

For the 1923 coinage of South Africa the mint established by Kruger in Pretoria was made a branch of the Royal Mint, London. Branches of the Royal Mint exist or have existed at one time or another in Ottawa, Pretoria, Calcutta, Bombay, Perth, Melbourne, Sydney, and Hong Kong. At the moment of writing it is not known if the new mint now established at Canberra to deal with the new Australian decimal coinage will be regarded as a branch of the Royal Mint, London. Certainly it has been announced that London will strike some of the new Australian coinage, since the change-over will need the immediate provision of a very large number of coins. Once the peak demand has been met the Canberra mint will probably be a separate mint on its own. One is glad that it is called The Royal Australian Mint.

The 50 Mazunas of Morocco (35), apparently dated 1289, brings us to a point which has confused many beginners. Here is an obviously modern coin which appears from its date to be of great antiquity.

All coins are not dated with the years of the Christian era. There are several other dating systems. A simple explanation of such dates on coins is given in the various editions of *A Catalog of Modern World Coins,* and we take the liberty of quoting it here.

'Most countries show the date more or less prominently on their coins. Little difficulty will be encountered with the coins of Europe, parts of Africa and the Americas. In the Arabic countries and countries of the near East and the Orient, however, strange symbols and letters pose a difficult problem of translation both of legends and dates.

'Countries using Arabic and Persian numerals observe the Mohommedan Era, also known as the Era of the Hegira (flight) using the letters A.H. In A.D. 622 Mohommed fled from Mecca to Medina, hence the era is reckoned from that date. To complicate date computation, these countries have at times used the lunar year of 354 days or about 3 per cent fewer days than our usual 365. To compensate for these factors, use the following formula to convert dates to the Christian (A.D.) Era.

Example: To convert 1330 A.H. into A.D. 3 per cent of 1330 = 39.90 (closest whole number is 40)

$$1330$$
$$-40$$
$$\overline{}$$
$$1290$$
$$+622$$
$$\overline{}$$
$$\text{A.D.} \quad 1912$$
$$\overline{}$$

'The coins of Siam use the dating system of two eras. The Buddhist Era (B.E.) which commenced in 543 B.C. can be converted into our own A.D. dates by subtracting 543. Four numerals will be found on current issues.

'The Bangkok Era (R.S.) dates from A.D. 1782. The A.D. dates would be computed by adding 1782 to the Bangkok date. Siamese coins of this era have three numeral dates.

'Several different eras were observed on the coinage of the India Native States.

'The Vikrama Era has its initial point in 57 B.C. and is observed mainly in Northern India. This is also known as the Samvat Era. Their year 1957 is our A.D. 1900.

'The Saka Era originated in the south-west corner of Northern India is the dominant era and the great historical reckoning of Southern India. It dates from A.D. 78. For example, Saka 1823 began in A.D. 1900.

'Chinese dates are correctly read from right to left. Coins of the Republic, when dated, start with the year A.D. 1912. Unlike our own system, coins of the Chinese Empire are dated according to a 60-year (sexagenary) cycle.'

To continue glancing over the plates again, coin (36), the 10 Cents of the Seychelles Islands, is another unusual shape, though somewhat more common than the square shape referred to above. Serrated coins of this type were used in India as stated above during the latter part of the Empire coinage.

The Seychelles, a group of islands in the Indian Ocean, 600 miles from Madagascar, had no coinage of its own under British rule until 1939, when an issue, based on the Rupee, commenced. The Rupee, regarded essentially as an Indian coin, has found its way either in fact or as a denomination, into many parts of the world. Indian Rupees have been used as far away as Australia before that country had its own coinage.

Before 1939 the Seychelles used the coins of other countries, mainly India. Before that, objects such as shells, fish hooks, and similar items regarded locally as of value were probably used as money. Such objects as these have come to be known as 'curious currency'. This subject, covering anything that has been used as money apart from coins, has inspired a most erudite and readable book, *A Survey of Primitive Money*, by Mrs Hingston Quiggin. Primitive money is a fascinating subject in itself, but apart from our present work.

Another fact should be mentioned stemming from our reference to the Seychelles. As European influence expanded and European navigators and traders 'discovered' the rest of the world, they found countries which were often in a high state of civilisation, where trade on an international scale had been going on for centuries. Some of these countries already had a coinage, others had not. In some cases where countries were populated by inhabitants who traded among themselves and who had not ventured far from their own shores, 'curious currency' was often found to be in use.

As the European maritime traders arrived a very considerable mixture of coins began to come into use in such countries. In cases where the Europeans 'took over' the country, by one method or another, a local currency based on European models frequently appeared in due time. Instances are South Africa, the Straits Settlements, the East Indies (Dutch and British), Hong Kong, Australia, and New Zealand.

Examples of mixtures of coinages becoming acceptable occurred in many such places, South Africa, the East Indies and Australia being good examples. In the former all sorts of miscellaneous coins, mainly European and Indian, were used for purposes of trade before the first issues of President Kruger laid the foundation for a local coinage.

In Australia when the Europeans began to settle, all sorts of European coins were used, together with Indian pieces, and such 'curious currency' as rum, Cape brandy, gold dust and grain. So far as the miscellaneous coins were concerned a list had to be drawn up showing equivalent values. No local currency had existed, since the country was so sparsely populated. Little or no trade existed with outside countries, save along the northern and western coasts, where contact was made with South-East Asia. Before Australian local currency was instituted in 1910 there were added to the mixture the many traders' token coins, private issues to facilitate trade, not a few of these being struck in Britain.

In the early days of Australian history, British currency was imported in what was thought to be sufficient quantities for use before the solution of the coinage problem in 1910. Edward VII died in the year when this local coinage was produced. The issue was, therefore, a short one and examples of the Edward VII coinage, especially in good condition, are now scarce. The Perth, Melbourne, and Sydney mints were set up to strike Australian coinage, Sydney closing again in 1925.

A moment of thought about what has been said concerning the circulation in a country of mixed money from many sources will show how such a piece as the Maria Theresa Thaler, with which this chapter started, comes to be recognised as a trading piece and acceptable among local traders, provided there is a sufficient quantity available for all to be familiar with it.

Perhaps a good example of how a country's coinage develops under colonisation and settlement can be seen from a look at Canadian coins, of which the silver Dollar is number 37 in the plates. A concise brief history is given by J. E. Charlton in his annual *Standard Catalogue of Canadian Coins, Tokens and Paper Money*, and we quote part of it here:

'Many collectors of Canadian coins commence their study at the point where folders and albums begin, the year 1858.' (Folders, punched and dated to take the various Canadian denominations are available. We have already mentioned albums.) 'This is the point when a 'decimal' coinage, based upon a dollar of 100 cents became the lawful exchange medium in the Province of Canada, replacing British sterling and a hodge-podge of foreign and private issues. It is the year when sizeable shipments of big bronze cents and silver 5-cent and 20-cent pieces arrived from London's Tower Mint to set the style for what was to be Dominion of Canada coinage. These large shipments of 1858 coinage, supplemented by nine million additional cents dated 1859, proved sufficient to meet the needs of the Colony until after Confederation (1867) and the first coins of the federal union, the 1870 strikings, retained the characteristics of the 1858 provincial issue. The silver 'fifth' (20 cents) was dropped, and replaced by the 25 cents, and the big 50-cent piece was inaugurated. The fine portraiture and attractive lines of the series which ensue naturally commend them to the new collector, and his familiarity with the denominations and main varieties makes him feel 'at home' in his collecting. Earlier Canadian 'money' consisted largely of private copper Tokens and British and foreign silver and gold, supplemented at times by private scrip and by the paper money of no less than 98 note-issuing banks. The tokens prove particularly interesting to the student and collector, and the fact that such a diversity of them remains accessible and inexpensive leaves no reason why the historic series should be ignored.

'A coin is backed by government authority. A token, on the other hand, may be the issue of a bank, firm, or individual, and exists only because it fills a somewhat local monetary need. It circulates; doing so, it becomes money in the full economic sense. Canada has, through necessity, had great need of such tokens, for under the French regime and the English, little money circulated or stayed in the New World. The early *Habitant* was largely self-sufficient, and barter could serve most of his needs.

But such growing urban centres as Halifax, St John, Quebec, Montreal and Toronto required money, and gold and silver tended to flow out of the Colonies faster than it could be brought in. A cosmopolitan diversity of gold, silver and copper pieces passed through the tills of the seaports, but the total in the Colonies at any given time was quite small. Prince Edward Island's 'holey dollar', the Milled Dollar of Spain with its centre punched out would not be accepted for international trade. A similar situation existed with the 'playing card money' of the French regime. In short, tokens had the advantage of staying where they were issued, and to that extent were a complete success. The advertising and political slogans of these series are fascinating – "Encourage Country Importers", "Fishery Rights for Newfoundland", "Pure Copper preferable to Paper", "No Labour – No Bread", "Speed the Plough". Glance through the illustrations, the political tokens, the interesting "bouquet sous", and the price listings, and you will see a series from which a remarkable and inexpensive selection can be made. Add to these the unbelievable mixture of world coinage once found in Canadian circulation, and still unearthed from time to time in Canada's more historic regions, and you have the picture of the nation's money prior to introduction of decimal coinage in 1858. A far cry from today! Yet it is not too long ago to remember when British halfpenny pieces circulated as cents, which they resembled, and the occasional shilling which passed at 25 cents, though it rated only 24, this as recently as World War II.'

Incidentally, an odd story lies behind the Canadian silver Dollar. Though the coinage was based on it, it was many years before dollars were actually struck. When the coinage was being prepared for the new reign in 1910–11, George V, the design for a silver dollar made its appearance as an illustration in the annual Report of the Royal Mint. The coin failed to appear, but speculation started concerning the possibility of a few proofs having been struck. After all it had been photographed, though the picture could have been made from a cast prepared from the dies, or from the plaster model prepared by the artist or from his designs.

In 1935, to mark the jubilee of King George V, the silver dollar at last made its appearance, but not to the design already published. It was as number (37) in the plates. The obverse showed a bust design said to have been evolved for Commonwealth coin obverses for this 25th anniversary year. Readers will have noted that it, or a bust very like it, had already appeared in 1932 in Southern Rhodesia, 33.

The reverse of the 1935 Dollar showed a trapper and an Indian in a canoe against the background of the forest pines and the northern lights. Apart from commemorative issues this reverse has remained constant.

Then about five years ago a 1911 Dollar appeared on the market, exactly as shown in the Mint Report. How many there may be no one knows. Only the one has so far appeared. Natuarally it changed hands at a considerable price, and is now in a collection.

In our family tree of the British coinage we mentioned the Fourpence or Groat. We illustrate another (40) struck at the Royal Mint, in silver, for British Guiana. We also illustrate the Florin of Fiji (41), dated 1964. Britain's first attempt at a decimal coinage (see 'family tree' page 33ff.) was to have repercussions here, as in South Africa, Australia and New Zealand, all of which countries issued a 'one tenth of a pound'.

Coin number 42 is the Penny of New Guinea, a territory which also had its own local coinage from 1935 till 1943 when Australian coinage replaced it. The initials below the central hole will be noted.

Sitting in his office one afternoon in 1936 the author received a parcel of new issues by air from Rabaul, the capital of New Guinea. Turning them over almost idly before putting them into the new issues cabinet he suddenly spotted that the cypher on the Penny was ERI. The first coin of Edward VIII had arrived. What made it interesting was that it already seemed probable that the King (Edward VIII) would never be crowned, as indeed turned out to be the case.

Subsequently East Africa, British West Africa, and Fiji also put minor denominations of Edward VIII coinage into circulation. All of them had the central hole, so none showed the portrait of the King.

It was because of this that the coins could be struck at all, since there was a difference of opinion between the king and the authorities as to which way the royal effigy should face. Long tradition decreed that each monarch should face in the opposite direction to his predecessor. For personal reasons Edward VIII wished to face in the same direction as his father. How the tradition arose probably no one knows, though various reasons are given. Possibly it was done in past centuries to help a less educated public to recognise the new coinage while it was in circulation with the coinage of the previous reign.

In any case the home coinage had not been proclaimed so that, in the event, as has been stated, only the few unofficial Threepences and the set of patterns were struck showing the King's head. So the humble colonial minor denominations listed above gained a collector's interest which they have never lost. None is really rare as quite considerable numbers were struck. But they have become scarce since World War II and all the changes that have followed it. The original New Guinea Penny can, perhaps, now be considered rare.

Stories, stories! They could be told for ever. Yet we have but touched the fringe with the few coins illustrated.

CHAPTER SEVEN

Where Coins can be seen

Coins of themselves are not simple things to display in an impressive manner. They need to be studied closely, and are therefore not at their best under glass in a museum. A visitor to the average museum may, therefore, be disappointed at not finding a display of coins.

A great deal of thought has been given to such displays by museum authorities, as by many others. Allied to maps, time charts, historical pictures and the like, coins can be brought to life and something of their interest expressed. Great care is needed with such displays, or the background will swamp the coins.

It has to be remembered that the study of coins is a part of history and archaeology, of social science, of the migration of peoples and of the rise and fall of nations: in fact, of world history. Some historical facts have only been proved by the evidence of coins; some rulers are known to have existed only because of the coins struck during their regime. Over long periods of time the most durable record of history is the coin. It will survive while buildings fall and written records perish. A great deal still has to be written about coins, particularly about ancient coins and the history they embody. Numberless numismatic problems have to be solved and lines of thought and deduction carried through to their logical conclusion, the coins themselves acting as the foundation stone. It is in the leading museum collections that a great deal of this work is done.

The museums that have large collections of coins generally

confine their display to a very small portion of the whole. Even the coins shown are often electrotype copies, since rare coins are tempting and easily stolen. The bulk of the collection is usually held in cabinets in a special coin room, both for reasons of security and for study.

The Department of Coins and Medals in the British Museum is a case in point. You might pass its doors almost without noticing them. Nothing but a modest doorbell marked 'Coins and Medals' gives a clue to what lies beyond the double doors. Since the gallery in which a display of coins and medals will one day reappear is still under reconstruction after war damage, there is little at the British Museum to inform the collector that there are any coins at all. Nothing but a modest showcase in the Edward VII gallery, a showcase or two on the mezzanine above the doors of the Department, and some cases of curious currency and coin weights and scales in the 'temporary' connecting passage between the Edward VII gallery and the main building give a clue to the national collection.

Yet beyond the bell marked 'Coins and Medals' lies one of the largest, richest, and most varied collections of coins in the world. It is a collection that numismatists and scholars travel the world to see and to study in connection with many types of numismatic and historical problems and research. Plaster casts of coins in the collection are sent out all over the world for study, for reference, and for photographing for illustrating books on coins. Many such casts were used to illustrate this book. The daily post received by the Department of Coins and Medals contains to many letters, from the enquirer with an odd coin to be identified, to the historian who poses some question that only research and reference can answer.

If, having found the bell, you still have the courage to ring it, you will be invited into a modern reception hall. The department, but fortunately not the collection, was a war casualty, and has recently been rebuilt in a pleasingly restrained modern style. If your enquiry needs nothing more than the identification of a single coin, or the answer to a simple question, an Assistant Keeper will come and deal with it. If your business needs more serious attention, you will be asked to sign the Visitors Book, and will be ushered through the heavy steel-bar door into the Coin Room proper, and securely locked in.

You are now surrounded by the cabinets containing the famous collection, and by the many books dealing with all phases and every period of coins and medals. Almost certainly there will be one or two students seated at the long U-shaped desk, carrying out some programme of research. If you wish to see any part of the collection it will be shown to you, under the watchful eyes of the staff. Coins are too easily stolen, too easily substituted, for any risks to be taken. Strange as it may seem, coin collecting can get such a grip that some otherwise quite honest and respectable people cannot resist the temptation to steal some much desired piece. One is conscious, therefore, of unobtrusive but watchful eyes, and of maximum security in the quiet atmosphere of the Department.

Like much of the other material in the British Museum, the coin collection is based on that of Sir Hans Sloane, whose historic collection went to form the nucleus of the Museum as a whole. The Royal collection also forms a basic part of the Department's holdings. Famous collections have been donated or purchased, coins are bought from all parts of the world. Single gift specimens are no less gratefully acknowledged than whole collections, and coins are acquired under the law of Treasure Trove. In these and other ways the collection is constantly growing.

Another large and important collection is to be seen at the Ashmolean Museum, Oxford. Here, in the Heberden Coin Room is a collection of importance equal to that at the British Museum. The visitor may see some fine examples of coins displayed in showcases, and members of the staff will accompany visitors round the display and answer any questions. Here again students will be found at work, and the staff busy with cataloguing and research. Here again, too, the collection is constantly being added to by gifts, purchases, and so forth. Each year's *Annual Report of the Visitors,* the official publication dealing with the activities and acquisitions of the museum, shows a record of the coins that have been added to the collection during the year under review. At the Ashmolean Museum is also a fine library of books on the whole subject of numismatics, and like other similar libraries such as that at the Department of Coins and Medals, British Museum, it is kept up to date by the addition of all worthwhile new publications. It was recently rehoused in a fine new library, ingeniously contrived within the Heberden Coin Room.

Yet another great collection is to be found at the Fitzwilliam Museum, Cambridge. Here, behind a solid door let into the wall of one of the galleries, a door which you might well pass unnoticed save for the showcase of coins hard by, lies a further collection of international importance. Here, as before, coins may be seen, questions answered, and programmes of study undertaken. Work goes on steadily and quietly, day after day, year after year. Not many University students submit a thesis on numismatics, yet it is a subject that affects much that is studied in a university. The thought is commended to their attention. At least it would have originality.

Perhaps less well-known is the collection of coins and material concerned with coin making which is housed at the Royal Mint. By reason of the place in which it is and the way it has been formed, this collection contains some unique material. It is a record of the activities of the Mint, and thus contains much that cannot be seen elsewhere. Small parties, usually of not more than three or four persons, may be shown round the Mint by arrangement. Application should be made to the Deputy Master for permission. Not only may the collection be seen but the whole process of modern minting will be shown to the visitor. One point will not escape him. Besides minting coins for Britain, he will be impressed by the enormous amount of money being struck for Commonwealth countries and for foreign governments. In fact the Royal Mint is a large and very successful business, with a high export record, and all sorts of coins may be seen in various stages of production.

In the University of Glasgow there exists the large collection of coins gathered together by the famous eighteenth century physician, anatomist, and medical teacher, William Hunter. This fine collection also has additions made to it from time to time. As with Hans Sloane, coins were not the only things Hunter collected, as may be seen by viewing the contents of the Hunterian Museum. So important is the collection of coins that it could rank as a national collection on its own. Its coverage is extremely wide, and many rarities are to be found. To give some idea how such great collections come into being, and of the munificence of Hunter himself, we quote the following extract from Miss Anne Robertson's catalogue of the Anglo-Saxon Coins (part 1) in the Hunterian and Coats Collections, University of Glasgow.

'In 1770 Hunter founded his own Theatre of Anatomy in a house newly built to his design at 16, Great Windmill Street, near what is now Piccadilly Circus.' (The site is now marked by one of the familiar L.C.C. blue plaques, let into the wall at the back of a theatre.) 'Besides his own residential quarters, the house contained dissecting rooms, a lecture theatre, a library, and a museum. The library and museum he steadily enriched and increased by discriminating purchases and sometimes by gifts presented by his many distinguished friends and patients. In this way he added to the purely medical collections, during the years 1770–1783, zoological and geological specimens, ethnographical and archaeological material, manuscripts and early printed books, paintings, and coins.

' "In making my collection." William Hunter said, "I have

44 William Wyon's magnificent design for a Five Pound, or Crown piece of Queen Victoria, 1839. Usually known as the 'Una and the Lion', the reverse shows Victoria as Una, guiding the British Lion. It is said that the design was not accepted since it was thought to be too medallic. Remembering what has been said about the way in which coins are damaged almost before they leave the mint, the beautiful high relief of the reverse would certainly soon have been spoiled had the piece been put into general circulation. **45** Few pattern pieces exist in the British series before 1662, when the whole coinage was redesigned and produced by primitive machinery. This pattern crown of 1663 is another design that was never put into production for general use, though it is very similar to the design actually accepted. The piece illustrated was designed by Thomas Simon, and the edge, which defies illustration, was inscribed with the legend, THOMAS SIMON MOST HUMBLY PRAYS YOUR MAJESTY TO COMPARE THIS HIS TRYALL PIECE WITH THE DUTCH AND IF MORE TRULY DRAWN AND EMBOSSED MORE GRACEFULLY ORDERED AND MORE ACCURATELY ENGRAVED TO RELIEVE HIM. This long legend was placed in two lines round the thin edge of the coin. It was Simon's protest against the designs for the new milled coinage being accepted from a Dutch artist, Roettier. **46** Very many designs seem to have been considered before the so-called 'Gothic' Florin (here illustrated) was accepted. After the 'Godless' Florin, already illustrated, this piece went into general circulation, and ousted the Half Crown for some 20 years. An enlarged and even more complex version of the 'Gothic' Florin theme became the 'Gothic' Crown, which probably never circulated. The many pattern Florins struck from designs not accepted could, and have, formed a fine and valuable collection of themselves. **47** The Crown of 1951. Struck to mark the centenary of the Great Exhibition of 1851, the Festival of Britain of 1951 and the 400th anniversary of the first English silver Crown of 1551. Some of these Crowns were struck at a Branch Mint on South Bank, then the Festival site. The pieces struck there have, unfortunately, no distinguishing mark. They were carefully struck and could be classified as proofs. In the light of later events, referred to in the text, they are probably more accurately classified as specimen pieces. **48** In more recent times a new class of piece, neither proof nor pattern, has been struck in the British Commonwealth. This 1965 Canadian Dollar is an example of such a piece. Carefully struck and highly polished, it contains none of the blemishes shown on the 'Churchill' Crown previously illustrated. To such pieces as this Dollar the term 'Specimen' has come into use as a term of condition description. The 1951 Crown just illustrated might also be placed in this category. **49** For the Trade Fair, held in New York in 1960, Crowns were struck at the Royal Mint on Tower Hill and exported. This is one of the pieces. Its design is that intended for use when ever a Crown piece might be struck after the coronation

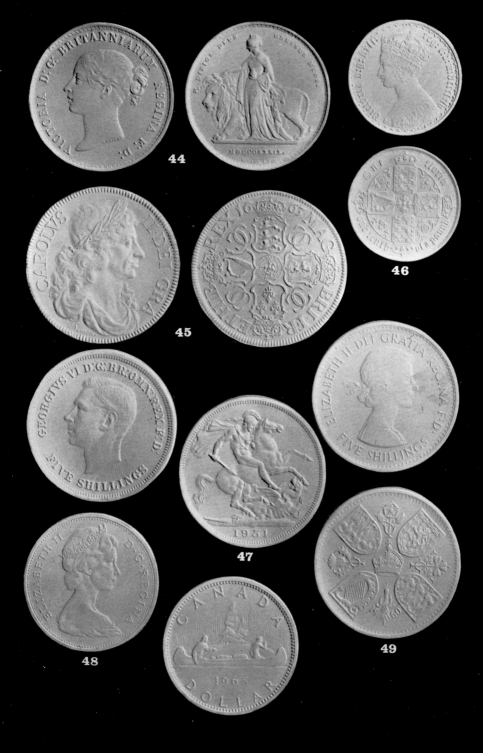

50

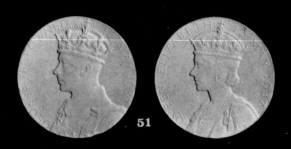

51

52

had the public in view", and during his lifetime while the museum was part of his house he made its treasures freely accessible to all who sought knowledge. By his will, he bequeathed his collections, as a teaching instrument, to the College of Glasgow, together with a sum of £8,000 towards their maintenance.

'In 1807 they were transported from London to Glasgow by sea – all except the coins. The coins travelled by road in a wagon escorted by "six trusty men accustomed to the use of arms".

'The accounts kept by William Hunter, still preserved in the Hunter Coin Cabinet, show that between 1770 and his death in March 1783, he spent between £22,000 and £23,000 on the purchase of coins, less about £2,000 recovered from the sale of duplicates.'

There is no need to calculate what these figures equal today. They are large enough in themselves. Thus the building up of the grand type of collection on which a national collection can be, and often is, founded. We have seen a collection on this scale even in our own time, that of the late Richard Cyril Lockett (1873–1950). In this case, while the collection was always available for study during his lifetime, the collector wished it to be sold at his death so that others might have the pleasure of owning some of the many choice pieces it contained. These, no less than the more humble coins in the collection, will always carry with them

50 The large Roman gold medallion, part of the famous Arras Treasure. The pictorial scene on the reverse is of the greatest interest. The technical skill needed to produce so fine a piece about 2,000 years ago is quite remarkable. Note the 'White Tower' on the right. **51** The not very imaginative design of the last of a long line of official Coronation Medals which started with James I, 1603–1625. This piece was struck for the coronation of George VI, and was offered in two sizes (of which this is the smaller), and three metals, gold, silver and bronze. **52** A crown piece, struck from the silver captured at the Battle of Vigo Bay, 1702. Note the word VIGO below the bust of Queen Anne the pedigree, 'ex Lockett collection'. Both national and private collections are now the richer by such additions. Under the hammer the collection realised some £300,000.

Further great collections exist at the Royal Scottish Museum, Edinburgh, the National Museum of Antiquities, Edinburgh, the Public Library and Museum, Salford, the Grosvenor Museum, Chester, the Museum, Manchester University, Bradford Museum, Trinity College, Dublin, the museums of Belfast, Bristol, Leeds, Birmingham, and many more.

Naturally not all these collections are on so vast a scale as those detailed above, but they are all of considerable importance and frequently contain some surprises.

Almost every museum in the country has a few coins of local interest. The Smith Institute, Stirling, has a collection of local seventeenth century tokens, while the Aylesbury Museum has an almost complete set of the same series of the County of Buckinghamshire.

Earlier in this book the Yearbook of the British Association of Numismatic Societies, *Cunobelin*, was mentioned. In the 1965 edition a list entitled 'Coin Collections in English Museums' was published, with some notes on the scope of the collections. In the interests of where coins can be seen the following list of museums is published. It does not contain the fuller details which can be found in the work from which it is compiled, and to which grateful acknowledgment is made for its pioneering work in this field:

ABINGDON, Borough Museum, Old County Hall, Abingdon, Berks.

AMPLEFORTH (YORK), College Museum, Ampleforth College, York.

ASHWELL, Village Museum, Ashwell, near Baldock, Herts.

AVEBURY, Museum, Avebury, Nr. Marlborough, Wilts.

BARROW-IN-FURNESS, Public Library, Ramsden Square, Barrow-in-Furness, Lancs.

BASINGSTOKE, Willis Museum, New Street, Basingstoke, Hants.

BATH, Roman Baths Museum, Bath.

BATH, Victoria Art Gallery, Bath.

BATH, Kingswood School, Bath.

BATLEY, Bagshaw Museum and Art Gallery, Wilton Park, Batley, Yorks.

BERWICK, Art Gallery and Museum, Marygate, Berwick-upon-Tweed.

BEVERLEY, Public Library, Art Gallery and Museum, Champney Road, Beverley, Yorks.

BLACKBURN, Museum and Art Gallery, Blackburn, Lancs.

BOGNOR REGIS, Museum Collection, c/o. Clerk of the Council, Town Hall, Bognor Regis, Sussex.

BOLTON, Museum and Art Gallery, Civic Centre, Bolton, Lancs.

BOOTLE, Art Gallery and Museum, Central Library, Oriel Road, Bootle, Lancs.

BOURNEMOUTH, Natural Science Society Museum, 39 Christchurch Road, Bournemouth.

BRADFORD, Cartwright Memorial Hall Museum, Bradford 9.

BRADFORD, Bolling Hall Museum, Bradford 4.

BRENTFORD, Public Library, Boston Manor Road, Brentford, Middlesex.

BRIDGWATER, Admiral Blake Museum, Blake Street, Bridgwater, Somerset.

BRIDLINGTON, Bayle Museum, Bridlington, Yorks.

BRIDPORT, Borough Museum, South Street, Bridport, Dorset.

BRIGHOUSE, Public Library and Art Gallery, Halifax Road, Brighouse, Yorks.

BRISTOL, City Museum, Queen's Road, Bristol 8.

BURY, Museum, Manchester Road, Bury, Lancs.

BURY ST. EDMUNDS, Moyses Hall Museum, Bury St. Edmunds, Suffolk.

BUXTON, Museum, Buxton, Derbyshire.

CASTLEFORD, Castleford Museum Room, Library and Museum, Castleford, Yorks.

CHELTENHAM, College Museum, Bath Road, Cheltenham.

CHESTER, Grosvenor Museum, Chester.

CHESTERFIELD, Public Library and Museum, Corporation Street, Chesterfield, Derbyshire.

CHINGFORD, Epping Forest Museum, Queen Elizabeth's Hunting Lodge, Rangers Road, Chingford, Essex.

CHRISTCHURCH, Red House Museum, Quay Road, Christchurch, Hants.

CLUN, Trust Museum, Town Hall, Clun, Shropshire.

CORBRIDGE, Corstopitum Roman Museum, Corbridge, Northumberland.

CRICKLADE, The Old Weigh House, Cricklade, Wilts.

DARLINGTON, Museum, Tubwell Row, Darlington, Co. Durham.

DARTFORD, Borough Museum, Central Park, Dartford, Kent.

DERBY, Museum, Wardwick, Derby.

DEVIZES, Museum, Long Street, Devizes, Wilts.

DEWSBURY, Museum, Crownest Park, Dewsbury, Yorks.

DONCASTER, Museum and Art Gallery, Doncaster, Yorks.

DORCHESTER, County Museum, Dorchester, Dorset.

DUDLEY, Museum, St James' Road, Dudley, Worcs.

DURHAM, The Cathedral Library, Durham.

ELSTOW, Moot Hall, Elstow, Beds.

ERITH, Borough Museum, Walnut Tree Road, Erith, Kent.

FARNHAM, Pitt-Rivers Museum, Farnham, Blandford, Dorset.

FOLKESTONE, Museum and Art Gallery, Grace Hill, Folkestone, Kent.

GATESHEAD, Saltwell Park Museum, Saltwell Towers, Gateshead 8, County Durham.

GLASTONBURY, Glastonbury Lake Village Museum, Glastonbury, Somerset.

GLOUCESTER, City Museum, Brunswick Road, Gloucester.

GODALMING, Museum, Charterhouse, Godalming, Surrey.

GRANTHAM, Public Library, Grantham, Lincs.

GRIMSBY, Doughty Museum, Town Hall Square, Grimsby, Lincs.

HALIFAX, Bankfield Museum, Halifax, Yorks.

HARROGATE, Royal Pump Room Museum, Crescent Road, Harrogate, Yorks.

HASTINGS, Museum, Hastings, Sussex.

HAYES, Hayes and Harlington Museum, County Library, Golden Crescent, Hayes, Middlesex.

HELSTON, Borough Museum, Helston, Cornwall.

HEREFORD, Museum, Broad Street, Hereford.

HEXHAM, Clayton Memorial Museum (generally known as Chesters Museum), Humshaugh, Hexham, Northumberland.

HIGH WYCOMBE, Museum, High Wycombe, Bucks.

HITCHIN, Museum, Paynes Park, Hitchin, Herts.

HOVE, Museum of Art, New Church Road, Hove, Sussex.

HUDDERSFIELD, Tolson Memorial Museum, Ravensknowle Park, Huddersfield.

HULL, Municipal Museums, 23/24, High Street, Kingston-upon-Hull.

ILKLEY, The Manor House, Museum, Ilkley, Yorks.

KEIGHLEY, Cliffe Castle Art Gallery and Museum, Keighley, Yorks.

KIDDERMINSTER, Museum, Market Street, Kidderminster, Worcs.

KINGSTON-UPON-THAMES, Museum, Fairfield Road, Kingston-upon-Thames, Surrey.

LANCASTER, Museum, Old Town Hall, Market Square, Lancaster.

LEEDS, City Museum, Park Row, Leeds 1, Yorks.

LEIGH, Pennington Hall Museum and Art Gallery, Leigh, Lancs.

LEICESTER, City Museum and Art Gallery, New Walk, Leicester.

LETCHWORTH, Museum and Art Gallery, Broadway, Letchworth, Herts.

LICHFIELD, Public Library, Art Gallery and Museum, Bird Street, Lichfield, Staffs.

LICHLADE (GLOS.), Filkins and Broughton Museum, Filkins, near Lichlade, Glos.

LINCOLN, City and County Museum, Broadgate, Lincoln.

LONDON, The Cuming Museum, Walworth Road, S.E.17.

LONDON, The Museum, Gunnersbury Park, W.3.

LONDON, Church Farm House Museum, Church End, Hendon, N.W.4.

LONDON, The Horniman Museum, Forest Hill, London, S.E.23.

LONDON, Islington Central Library, 68 Holloway Road, N.7.

LONDON, Mocatta Museum, University College, Gower Street, W.C.1.

LONDON, Sir John Soane's House, 13 Lincoln's Inn Fields, W.C.2.

LONDON, Southgate Museum, Broomfield Park, Palmer's Green, N.13.

LONDON, Woolwich Borough Museum, 232 Plumstead High Street, Plumstead, S.E.18.

LOUGHBOROUGH, Museum, Granby Street, Loughborough.

LYME REGIS, Philpot Museum, Lyme Regis, Dorset.

MACCLESFIELD, Macclesfield Museum, Hare Hill, Macclesfield, Cheshire.

MAIDSTONE, The Museum and Art Gallery, St Faith Street, Maidstone, Kent.

MALVERN, Public Library, Graham Road, Malvern, Worcs.

MANCHESTER, Museum, University of Manchester 13.

MANSFIELD, Museum and Art Gallery, Leeming Street, Mansfield, Notts.

MARKET HARBOROUGH, Archaeological and Historical Society, County Library, The Square, Market Harborough.

MATLOCK, Heathcote Museum, Birchover, Matlock, Derbyshire.

NEWARK-ON-TRENT, Municipal Museum, Appleton Gate, Newark-on-Trent, Notts.

NEWBURY, Borough Museum, Newbury, Berks.

NEWCASTLE-UPON-TYNE, Society of Antiquaries of Newcastle, Black Gate Museum, Newcastle-upon-Tyne.

NOTTINGHAM, City Museum and Art Gallery, The Castle, Nottingham.

NUNEATON, Museum and Art Gallery, Riversley Park, Nuneaton, Warwickshire.

OLDHAM, Municipal Art Gallery and Museum, Union Street, Oldham, Lancs.

PENZANCE, Penlee Museum, Morrab Road, Penzance.

POOLE, Museum, South Road, Poole, Dorset.

ROBERTSBRIDGE, Bodiam Castle, Bodiam, Robertsbridge, Sussex.

ROCHDALE, Corporation Museum, Esplanade, Rochdale, Lancs.

ROTHERHAM, Municipal Museum, Clifton Park, Rotherham.

RUGBY, Borough Library and Museum, Rugby, Warwickshire.

RYE, Rye Museum, Watchbell House, Rye.

ST ALBANS, Verulamium Museum, St Michael's, St Albans, Herts.

ST HELENS, Public Museum, c/o. Central Library, St Helens, Lancs.

SALISBURY, Salisbury and S. Wilts Museum, Ann Street, Salisbury.

SANDOWN, I.O.W. Museum of Isle of Wight Geology, Sandown, I.O.W.

SEVENOAKS, Local Museum, Public Library, The Drive, Sevenoaks, Kent.

SHAFTESBURY, Local History Museum, Gold Hill, Shaftesbury, Dorset.

SHEFFIELD, Museum, Weston Park, Sheffield 10.

SHREWSBURY, Museum, Castle Gates, Shrewsbury.

SIDMOUTH, Museum, Woolcombe House, Woolcombe Lane, Sidmouth, Devon.

SKIPTON, Craven Museum, Skipton, Yorks.

SOUTHAMPTON, Tudor House Museum, St Michael's Square, Southampton.

SOUTHEND-ON-SEA, Prittlewell Priory, Southend.

SOUTH MOLTON, Museum, South Molton, Devon.

SOUTHPORT, Atkinson Art Gallery, Lord Street, Southport, Lancs.

SOUTHPORT, Botanic Gardens Museum, Churchtown, Southport, Lancs.

SOUTH SHIELDS, Public Library and Museum, Ocean Road, South Shields, Co. Durham.

STAFFORD, Museum, The Green, Stafford.

STOCKTON-ON-TEES, Preston Hall, Stockton-on-Tees, Co. Durham.

STOKE-ON-TRENT, Museums and Art Gallery, Broad Street, Hanley, Stoke-on-Trent, Staffs.

SUNDERLAND, Museum, Borough Road, Sunderland, Co. Durham.

TAMWORTH, Castle Museum, Holloway, Tamworth, Staffs.

TAUNTON, Somerset County Museum, Taunton Castle, Taunton.

THETFORD, Ancient House Museum, White Hart Street, Thetford, Norfolk.

TILBURY, Thurrock Local History Museum, Civic Square, Tilbury.

TUNBRIDGE WELLS, Municipal Museum, Mount Pleasant, Tunbridge Wells, Kent.

UXBRIDGE, County Library, High Street, Uxbridge, Middlesex.

WAKEFIELD, City Museum, Wood Street, Wakefield, Yorks.

WALSALL, Central Library and Art Gallery, Lichfield Street, Walsall, Staffs.

WELLS, Museum, Cathedral Green, Wells, Somerset.

WEST HARTLEPOOL, Gray Art Gallery and Museum, Clarence Road, Hartlepool, Co. Durham.

WHITBY, Museum, Pannett Park, Whitby, Yorks.

WINCHESTER, City Museum, Winchester, Hants.

WORKSOP, Public Library and Museum, Worksop, Notts.

YARMOUTH, Museum, 4 South Quay, Gt Yarmouth, Norfolk.

YEOVIL, Wyndham Museum, Yeovil, Somerset.

YORK, The Yorkshire Museum, York.

YORK, Castle Museum (Folk Museum of Yorkshire Life), York.

The coins, medals and tokens held by the museums listed above are as varied as can possibly be imagined. They include local finds, gifts, whole donated collections, and single specimens. Some of the museums are able to spend time and money on arranging or cataloguing their coins. Others cannot, though with the rising interest in coins as a whole they may soon wish to do so.

The Curator of a provincial museum has much to deal with. Quite apart from dealing with exhibitions as wide apart in subject as a collection of vintage motor cars, modern paintings, the local history of the past, and the local activities of the present, he may also have to work out the cost of running the museum for the next year or two, superintend a large staff from cleaners to night watchmen and, in his spare time, if any, scour the auction sale catalogues, and in many other ways keep his eyes open for additions to the collection in his charge. He may know nothing about coins. He might well use some unpaid help in cataloguing the coins he knows are somewhere in the museum.

Potential helpers should consult the full details given in

the list of museums in *Cunobelin*. Help in dealing with collections of coins by someone knowing something of the subject, and being himself a responsible person, might be very useful. The Curator of the Worksop Public Library and Museum submitted the following entry to the list in *Cunobelin*, 'Museum not opened since the war. The coin collection is a mixed one. If and when the museum is opened, help would be welcomed'. This gentleman may well have expressed the thoughts of others of his profession.

*

CHAPTER EIGHT

Pattern and Proof Coins

There are some collectors who have specialised, sometimes as a sideline to their main theme of collecting, in pattern and proof coins. Most collectors have some in their cabinets. They are a group of pieces slightly apart from normal coins, and as such deserve something said about them. The two types are quite distinct and should not be confused.

A pattern coin is struck from a design which is not eventually accepted as suitable for use for currency. Probably the best known pattern in the British series is the Five-Pound piece of Victoria, usually known as 'Una and the Lion'. A magnificent piece, designed by the famous William Wyon, it was considered to be too medallic for use as a currency piece. A limited number were struck, and the piece is highly prized by collectors. In this connection it can be said at once that pattern pieces are always rare, and that to collect many of them needs considerable wealth.

They are also one of the highest achievements of the moneyer's art, in that every piece is struck with very great care. The flan of the coin is polished, usually before striking, and the dies themselves are also polished. The patterns are struck one at a time, and are not allowed to damage themselves in any way, being removed from the machine with the greatest care. Even then they are sometimes given a final polish by hand. The result is a coin with the reflective value of a mirror. Naturally this finish shows to best advantage in gold, but silver and bronze patterns are almost equally effective in their attraction.

Proof pieces are struck in a similar manner and with equal care, from a design which is eventually accepted for currency issues. Here the number struck may vary very considerably.

Broadly speaking a few proof coins are struck every time any alteration is made to the design. Each year when the date of a coin in current use is changed in readiness for the next year's issue, a few pieces, thought to be about 25 in number, are struck as proofs at the Royal Mint. These, it is assumed, are inspected by the Chief Engraver, the Deputy Master, and Treasury officials directly connected with mint operation. It can thus be seen that all is well with the alteration. Some of these proofs are quite legitimately retained by their recipients. Some, regrettably from the collector's point of view, go back into the melting pot.

This was probably the beginning of the issue of proof coins: a practical demonstration of what the coin was going to look like when struck for daily use. It was soon realised that such pieces had a collector's interest. The idea then grew up that when a new coinage was being prepared, a limited number could be struck as proofs and offered for sale. These proofs usually consisted of a complete set of the coins of the realm, and they were offered to the public at a reasonable premium. Their appearance usually coincided with the coinage for a new reign, a royal celebration such as the 1887 Jubilee, or a re-design of coinage during the reign, as in 1927.

In Britain the production of such proof sets and single pieces has almost always been in very limited numbers. They are usually offered in a fine fitted leather case, where they can be seen to their best advantage. The collector has a set of coins whose production has not been overtaken by rampant commercialism. As an example, in 1937 when George VI was crowned, a limited number of proof sets of coins of the new reign were offered to the public. Such sets are now highly prized.

But it soon became apparent to some governments of the

world that, with the steady growth of collectors, there was a market for proof sets that could be very profitable. Some mints, therefore, started to issue proof sets every year. Though the issue is still limited, it does tend to be tied to the number of applications received so that, year by year, more and more such sets are produced.

Apart from this, countries just starting out with newly won independence saw a revenue from the issue of considerable numbers of proof sets. Even countries that never had any coinage of their own, or at best only a few minor denominations, are climbing on the band wagon and dreaming up proof sets of coins.

All this adds something to the collecting picture and places proof sets within the reach of many more collectors. But from the purely numismatic point of view the multiplication of the production of proofs does rather tend to take the edge off them and to render them just one more proof set.

Even so it has been done before. Boulton and Watt produced many fine proofs and patterns, both from their Soho mint and from the then modern minting machinery which they were supplying to foreign government mints. Later their Soho dies were to fall into other hands, resulting in the issue of restrikes, thus complicating the whole numismatic picture. Referring back to the catalogue of '*English Copper, Tin and Bronze Coins in the British Museum*', the reader of it will see what effort it cost the author to identify and separate these 'Soho restrikes' and place them in their own particular category.

Similarly with patterns. It has come to be realised that there is no bar to the private production of 'suggested patterns' for a coin or coins. Speculators have not been slow to cash in on this and to surround their products with the necessary cloak of protective wording as an insurance against possible prosecution. If the late Martin Coles Harman had struck his Puffin and Half Puffin coins as patterns for a Lundy coinage instead of insisting that they were his own local coinage for use on his privately owned island, he might never have seen the inside of a court of law.

The mint laws in India are different from those of many other mints. There the ancient custom has survived whereby anyone taking precious metal to the mint can have it converted into the equivalent value in coinage. It has recently been realised that under these circumstances if the metal is provided by the purchaser and he is willing to pay all the expenses, coins can be struck from any dies held at the Bombay mint. This has led to a number of proof and pattern pieces being struck from dies long since out of use or, in some cases, never officially used at all.

Such pieces certainly fill gaps in a collector's cabinet, but they have not the true ring of the genuine specimen, be it pattern, proof, or currency piece. They are later strikings, and have not the same significance. All of these matters will complicate the numismatic picture in years to come, when their origin has been forgotten. Meantime the true collector has to be on his guard against them.

The British Royal Mint has, therefore, issued a limited number of genuine patterns and proofs available to the collector. Few such pieces exist before 1662, when British coins began to be made in quantity by machinery. Even after this date such pieces are very rare but, as stated above, at the turn of the 18th century they began to appear with more frequency.

Before the Guinea was replaced by the Sovereign in 1817, struck on the new minting machines just supplied by Boulton and Watt, a number of fine pattern and proof pieces appeared. With the introduction of the reformed coinage, establishing the Sovereign, and with Pistrucci and the Wyons at work at the Royal Mint, many fine pieces were to be struck. Pattern and proof crowns of this period can be had, some of them of the greatest rarity. Extremely small numbers of proof sets appeared in the reigns of George IV (1820–1830), and

William IV (1830–1837), and some equally rare sets in the early days of Victoria.

With the agitation for a decimal coinage culminating in the issue of the Florin, some fine patterns and proofs of the new piece were produced. Very many designs seem to have been considered before the so-called 'Gothic' Florin was decided upon. In 1887 the Queen's Jubilee was marked by a much criticised new coinage, and this was issued in both proof and currency sets. Similar sets of the further redesigned coinage appeared in 1894. Proof sets of the new coinage of Edward VII were struck in 1902. In this case a frosted finish was given to the coins instead of the brilliant tone usually associated with patterns and proofs.

The years 1911 and 1937 both saw similar proof sets of the new coinage for the reign, finished in the traditional bright manner. The year 1950 saw a small set of proofs issued to mark the half century, and 1951 produced more proof sets and proof crowns. These latter were to mark the centenary of the Great Exhibition of 1851, the Festival of Britain, 1951, and the first introduction of the English silver crown in 1551. Of this 1951 issue the Crown is probably the commonest of the proofs struck by the Royal Mint. Some of them were struck and placed on sale at a small branch mint established on the Festival of Britain site, South Bank, London. Here they were produced more or less on demand and sold to visitors. The number issued was, therefore, a large one and the pieces found their way to many parts of the world very rapidly. Even so there was probably a pre-determined limit. A large striking of legal tender under such circumstances could conceivably affect the value of the pound.

The countries of the British Empire and the British Commonwealth of Nations produce proof pieces or sets from time to time, as stated above. These are struck either at the Royal Mint, by the branch mints which at one time or another have operated at Ottawa, Pretoria, Bombay, Calcutta, Hong Kong, Perth, Melbourne, and Sydney, or by private mints. Such private mints frequently act as sub-contractors to the Royal Mint. Such, as has been mentioned, was Boulton and Watt's mint at Soho, Birmingham, later Ralph Heaton and Son, now The Mint, Birmingham, Ltd, who normally place a letter H on their productions by way of mint mark. The earliest British and British Commonwealth proof pieces, as distinct from the speculative sets mentioned above, are becoming rarer as the collecting interest and the investment of money in rare coins increases. But the possession of just one such set can add a touch of glamour to a collection. The individual pieces serve to show what a coin can really look like when it has been well and carefully struck.

In more recent times a new class of piece, neither proof nor pattern, has been struck in the British Commonwealth,

53 When we come to such events as the building of our railways we often find detailed pictorial representations of such engineering achievements. This is one of several medals struck to commemorate the opening of the Liverpool and Manchester Railway, 1830. What ever may be said about the work of that tough old Northumbrian George Stephenson, the Liverpool and Manchester Railway was his personal achievement. With little or no education by modern standards, but with a vast reservoir of sound common sense, 'Old George' set the standard for the steam operated railways of the world. The minute detail shown on the reverse of this medal is typical of the 'picture medal' of the period. **54** Sir Isambart Marc Brunel, F.R.S., the man who started to dig the world's first underwater tunnel, which is still in use, beneath the River Thames. The reverse of this pictorial medal shows a section of the bore. Twenty years in the building, owing mainly to lack of text-book knowledge: the text-books not yet having been written: this pioneer tunnel was completed by Marc's son, I. K. Brunel, the most flamboyant of the Victorian railway engineers. 'I. K.' built the Clifton suspension bridge, the Great Western Railway, the 'Great Eastern' (a ship far in advance of her time), and other Victorian engineering marvels. He also swallowed a Sovereign by accident while entertaining children with a conjuring trick, and invented, on the spot, a method of recovering it before its presence could cause his death. **55** A modern commemorative medal, struck to mark the 50th anniversary of the building of the Simplon Tunnel. The obverse represents the efforts of the workers, hewing a tunnel through solid Alpine rock, while the reverse shows one of the portals of the tunnel

53

54

55

56

57

58

notably by Canada and South Africa, as well as in countries abroad. These pieces receive great care in production and are polished, usually after striking. To them the designation 'specimen coins' has been applied. Their numbers are usually limited only by the demand for them, which is considerable. They make an attractive addition to any collection.

As branch mints have frequently been mentioned, perhaps a word might be said about them here. Ottawa, Pretoria, Bombay, Calcutta, Hong Kong, Perth, Melbourne and Sydney mints were obviously set up to provide the coinage for the countries concerned. While in operation they are, or were, all official Branch Mints of the Royal Mint, Tower Hill. The coins which they struck had to be approved by the Royal Mint. The master punches from which the dies were prepared, or the master dies from which the working dies were manufactured, were usually sent out from the Royal Mint. The Hong Kong mint proved to be a financial failure, and was closed only a few years after commencing work, though it had time to produce some local coinage as well as

56 Commemorative medals have been given as awards. Such are Davison's medals. This medal is, then, something of a hybrid. It commemorates the Battle of Trafalgar, 1805, and was struck by Nelson's prize agent for those who took part in the action. Admirals received it in gold, lower ranks in silver and lower deck ratings in bronze; who mostly scorned it and threw it overboard. Had it been given attached to a brooch and riband in the modern style they would probably have worn their 'decoration' with pride. **57** 'The earliest instance we know of one (medal) commemorative of a particular event being evidently meant to be worn as an ornament is the Armada Medal.' (Mayo). Illustrated is one of several Armada Medals. Attached to a riband or silken cord it could be worn as a 'dress ornament'; a 'decoration'; just as today our ladies are liable to wear a clutch of gold coins or ornaments attached to a bracelet. Herein lies the origin of our modern system of military and civil decorations and awards. In another 400 years what will our present ladies bracelets have become? **58** Awarded for academic achievement. The obverse of the gold Sanford Saltus medal, awarded every three years by the British Numismatic Society for outstanding contribution to the science of numismatics. The reverse is engraved with the recipient's name and the year of the award quite a number of pattern and proof pieces. The two Indian mints were taken over by their own government when the country became independent. Sydney mint closed in 1925. Pretoria mint was taken over by the South African Government for use as their own mint.

All these were permanent Branch Mints, but there have also been temporary mints set up for various purposes. Under the British Coinage Acts if a coin is to be legal tender it can only be struck at the Royal Mint, at an official Branch Mint, or by sub-contractors to the Royal Mint. During the second World War machinery was removed from Tower Hill and set up at a temporary mint 'somewhere in the country'. Had the Royal Mint been destroyed by enemy action the vital production of coinage could still have been carried on.

As already stated, a small Branch Mint was set up on the Festival of Britain site on South Bank, London, in 1951. Though it confined its activities to the striking of Crown pieces dated 1951, it was an official mint, otherwise the Crowns struck would have been forgeries.

We have seen that the Royal Mint is a business. As such it solicits orders from foreign countries for its products. When the Trade Fair was held in New York in 1960 the Royal Mint had an exhibit, and was striking a special commemorative medal. A number of 1960 Crowns were struck in London, enclosed in a suitably inscribed plastic case and sold in New York. Not a few of the people who bought them seemed to think they had been struck by the machine they saw in operation. This could not be so, or a Branch Mint would have had to be opened in New York. One would assume that the only place where a Branch Mint could operate in America would be at the British Embassy.

CHAPTER NINE

Commemorative Medals

So far the main interest of this book has been with coins, but every so often the word medals has occurred. Very few works of introduction to numismatics have much to say about them. They are in fact a somewhat separate branch of the science.

There is a connection between coins and medals going back to at least Roman times. The Romans struck coins which commemorated some particular event or showed some particular person. They were soon striking commemorative medals. One of the most famous formed part of what is known as the Arras Treasure. This famous treasure, which takes its name from the find-spot, contained a large gold medal showing an interesting scene. Constantius Chlorus is shown on horseback, facing right. Before him is a kneeling figure with arms outstretched. Below the figure is the abbreviation LON, for London. In the foreground a Roman galley filled with soldiers is afloat on the Thames. What has always intrigued the author is the fact that the kneeling figure has behind it a fort, half of which is shown, whose design almost forecast the appearance of the present Tower of London since it bears something of the appearance of the White Tower, which in fact was not to be built for some centuries to come (*circa* A.D. 1072). Military architecture had not, apparently, changed so much in the interval. The subject of the whole little scene thus commemorated is the entry of Constantius Chlorus into London.

To return to the subject as a whole: a medal is usually considerably larger than a coin, though they come in all sizes. When larger than a coin the medal gives the artist more scope for his design, especially in respect of portraiture. In many cases the head of the monarch, or of some particular person of interest, occupies one side, usually the obverse. The purpose of the medal may be simply to perpetuate the personality thus portrayed. Conversely, he may have been the ruler at the time when some event of importance took place. In such a case the reverse is usually devoted to showing that event.

An example of the former type is the official coronation medal. Here the obverse is usually occupied by a fine portrait, somewhat stylised, of the monarch, while the reverse will contain, possibly, the royal arms, or a stylised representation of the act of coronation. From James I (1603–1625) to George VI (1936–1952) such a coronation commemorative medal was issued in Britain. In some cases two were issued, one being for the queen consort. In other cases more than one type was struck.

The second main type of medal was soon seized upon as a vehicle of propaganda, especially in times of war, and particularly before the invention of the newspaper, the radio, and the film. The reigns of William III (1694–1702) and Queen Anne (1702–1714) were one of Britain's most prolific periods of propaganda medal production. Readers may recall that this was the culminating period of a long series of wars against the French and the continental alliance. Many medals were struck marking various stages of the campaigns. One or two show Marlborough and Eugene, commanders whose names are known to every schoolchild.

Even here it is often the case that the obverse of a commemorative/propaganda medal shows a portrait of the monarch. The reverse usually tells the story of the event by way of allegory, or pictorial representation.

For example, when the government and people of Britain found it necessary to drive James II (1685–1688) from the throne and invite William of Orange to invade the country and restore the political and religious *status quo*, medals were struck to commemorate, among other stirring events, the landing of William at Torbay. A statue of him stands at Brixham to mark the spot where he landed.

The obverse of the medal shows a half-length portrait of William. The reverse shows his fleet approaching the coast. Troops are drawn up on the beach. Before them William, mounted on horseback and clad in armour, is directing operations. 'On to London', one can almost hear him say, much as some of our 'armies' of today might say 'On to Trafalgar Square'. In the foreground a warrior is reviving the fainting figure of Justice. Into all this can be read the story of the invasion.

Many of the commemorative medals of the history of the reign of James II make use of a lot of allegorical representations. The artists had a whole stock of thunderbolts, fierce eagles, all-seeing eyes, lightning flashes, falling buildings, broken columns, and so forth, which were used on appropriate occasions.

But while allegory is something of a stock form of representation among many medallic artists, others try to be more factual and to give a miniature picture of the events recorded. One could give many examples of both forms of treatment, but the story behind one of the latter may be of some interest.

In the reign of Queen Anne a fleet set out to raid Cadiz, as a part of the complex military and naval operations then being carried out in the war referred to above. For various reasons the raid failed. However, the commanders of the fleet learned, almost by chance, of the arrival of a great French and Spanish treasure fleet from the West Indies which was making for Vigo Bay.

Just as in the last war Hitler attempted to starve us out by cutting our maritime supply lines by submarine activities, so in this war the fleets hammered at each other on every possible occasion, and every attempt was made to bottle up the ships of the opposing nations. The capture of such a treasure fleet would not only be a considerable financial loss to the enemy, but the treasure could immediately be used to our own advantage to help pay for the war.

The treasure fleet succeeded in making Vigo Bay before the combined English and Dutch force came up with it. The Spanish fleet locked itself in Vigo Bay by placing a heavy boom across the narrow neck of the harbour entrance. This the allied fleet succeeded in forcing. The story of the action is told by Sir Winston Churchill in his *Marlborough*, which we quote:

'It was decided to raid the harbour. This was protected by a boom and batteries, behind which lay the enemy squadrons of forty-five vessels, including fifteen ships of the line. To reach them and their treasure it was necessary to break the boom and enter the long sleeve of a comparatively landlocked harbour under the heaviest fire from the shore. One writer has said of Rooke' (the Admiral in charge) 'that "he swooped down through the boom, struck panic into his foes, and overwhelmed them in destruction", another that "he lay in his berth, ill of the gout, far down the bay",' and Sir Winston adds a footnote 'certainly he took no active part in the execution of the plan.' 'On October 12 Vice-Admiral Hopson in the Torbay, followed by all but the heaviest English and Dutch battleships, braved the fire of the batteries, crashed through the boom, and penetrated the inner harbour. Here a fierce battle was fought with the French warships, while Ormonde with two thousand soldiers attacked the principal fort from the land. Whether the lure of gold, or the sting of Cadiz' (which was to have been partly a land operation, hence the soldiers), 'or both, inspired the leaders, at last they let loose their brave men, who fought with indomitable fury. By sundown they were masters of Vigo Bay. The entire enemy fleet was sunk, burned or captured. Not one escaped. The treasures of the Indies were frantically carried inland by mules before the action, but enough remained for the victors to bear home a million sterling to sustain the Treasury and appease Parliament.'

Even so it is still believed that much treasure went down with the ships, and attempts are made from time to time to locate it, with no success so far. Of the million that was sent to Britain, some was used for coinage. Pieces said to have been struck from this supply have the word VIGO on them, below the bust of Queen Anne. Gold coins of this type are rare: not much of this metal was captured. The silver coins are more common, though scarce.

A number of triumphant medals were struck to commemorate this battle. On many of them Queen Anne's bust occupies the obverse. The reverse usually shows a picture of the actual battle taking place in the confines of Vigo Bay, the part where the treasure fleet lay being shaped roughly like a figure 8 with the bottom curve removed. The varieties of this pictorial type medal can be seen in the National Maritime Museum collection.

One can but mention briefly the two very broad treatments so often used in commemorative medals. In the late 18th and through much of the 19th century the picture style of medal gained in appeal. In the time of Nelson and Wellington hollow medals were struck which, when opened, contained beautiful little circular aquatints picturing the campaigns, with the story of each printed on the reverse.

When we come to such events as the building of the British canal system and the early days of the building of our railways we often find very detailed pictorial representations of such engineering achievements. The growth of the newspaper no doubt had some influence at first towards the popularity of this type of medal. As foreshadowed by the hollow medals mentioned above, multiplication by printing and commercial colour work was on the increase. Though the camera had not yet been invented, newspapers began to look more like those which we know today and began to be available to more of the population, whose education in the three R's was increasing. Clever 'lightning' artists portrayed with pencil and pen events as they actually happened. Reference to the early files of such journals as the *Illustrated London News* will show to what heights these artists brought their work. People began to expect factual representations, and this was catered for in many of the medals of the 19th century.

Mechanical methods of coin and medal production increased the output of commemorative medals very considerably during the same period. With the increase came, in many instances, much inferior artistic work. The invention of the photograph and the film undoubtedly had the effect of decreasing some types of commemorative medal production. One could now see events as they happened, either in the popular press or by postcards showing some local scene, Later one could both see and hear events actually happening.

All this had the effect of returning the commemorative medal to a more exclusive position. Now, in the main, only events which were considered of sufficient importance to need permanent record in a more stable form than paper and celluloid became subjects for medals. Their artistic merit increased again till there are at the present time some fine medals being produced, both in this country and in Europe. A few years ago a fine exhibition of such medals was arranged, and toured many European cities, including London.

So far as the formation of private collections of commemorative medals is concerned, this has for some years been in decline, at any rate in Britain. There is little doubt that this was partly due to the fact that the British Museum catalogue, *The Medallic History of Great Britain* (etc.), terminates at the end of the reign of George II (1760). By the end of the reign of George III (1820), mechanical methods were beginning to increase production, as mentioned above. By the end of the reign of Queen Victoria (1901), so many medals had been struck that the task of any potential cataloguer had become immense,

The production by the late Leonard Forrer of the *Bio-graphical Dictionary of Medallists* (etc.), itself a task which took many years since its coverage is international, was of considerable importance. Having a medal to identify, and having found the artist responsible for the design, the history of the artist and further notes on his work could easily be found from the *Dictionary*. Only a very limited edition of this work of eight volumes was produced. With its passing out of print the want of records was again felt.

The late Colonel Grant, better known for his important standard work on English painters, collected modern medals for many years, with the intention of producing a catalogue. In the event nothing more than a list appeared in the British Numismatic Journal, and the matter again lapsed. His collection and the notes he made are now in the Ashmolean Museum, Oxford.

Within the last few years, however, interest has revived once more in medal collecting. Several factors may have contributed to this welcome revival. Fine coins are becoming somewhat scarcer with more people collecting, and there are more people now who take an interest in history.

It will be seen from what has been said that there are many fields of interest open to the medal collector. The present interest in investing money in gold in various forms has led to an almost Victorian spate of gold commemorative medals. There is already a movement on foot for bringing the *Biographical Dictionary of Medallists* up to date, and possibly for reprinting the original volumes. Events of importance continue to be recorded, the 900th Anniversary of Westminster Abbey being a case in point.

Personalities, social history, buildings, transport, wars, politics; the collector has all history before him in the commemorative medal, a field of reviving interest and one in which, be he so minded, much valuable recording work can be undertaken.

※

CHAPTER TEN

Decorations, Military and Civil

Military Decorations: usually referred to under the collective heading of 'war medals'; and Civil Decorations are one step further from coin collecting. They are indeed a separate subject. Even so, medals awarded for gallantry and service, both in war and civil life, have their connection through the commemorative medal in that in the past commemorative medals have been given as awards. Such are Davison's medals, which commemorate Nelson's naval actions, and a number of others looking very like the commemorative type have been used for wearing on the person as decorations.

Mayo, in his standard work on the subject, *Medals and Decorations of the British Army and Navy*, 1897, states:

'Although the practice of commemorating important events by medals is of ancient origin, the custom of making the medal serve a double purpose by using it as a decoration is comparatively modern. When or where the custom originated has not been ascertained.' He adds as a footnote: 'The Chinese, however, seem to have been an exception. Military medals are said to have been used during the Han dynasty, A.D. 10.'

He then continues, 'In England, although the wearing of medals was common in the reign of Henry VIII, the earliest instance we know of one commemorative of a particular event being evidently meant to be worn as an ornament, is the Armada Medal.

'British naval and military decorations may be classed generally under two heads:

(i) As rewards to particular individuals:
  (*a*) For personal valour
  (*b*) For generally meritorious behaviour.
(ii) As rewards for participation in battles or campaigns:
  (*a*) To commanders and superior officers
  (*b*) To officers and men alike.'

Thus we have summed up very briefly the development of medals as decorations, and the modern practice for which such decorations are awarded.

Although the East India Company decorated some of its servants with medals, suspended from ribands, similar to those with which we are now familiar, military and naval decorations as we know them may have said to have been started when a medal, awarded soon after the Battle of Waterloo, was instituted. In 1848 the Naval General Service medal was instituted in the form in which we know it today.

To quote Mayo again, 'Another feature of Her Majesty's reign has been the grant of medals to the survivors of those who participated in services, whether by sea or land, since 1793, which had not previously been so commemorated; and the survivors had therefore the satisfaction of receiving, albeit somewhat late in the day, the coveted reward for their services.'

This cleared up a back-log of people who ought to have been decorated for their services, and a moment's thought will discover in the above paragraph the seeds of our system of awarding decorations at the present time.

The descendants of the medals mentioned above can be seen today being worn at any military or important parade or function.

The practice of wearing part of the riband only, in the form of a bar, is usual on suitable occasions. Obviously a person cannot be very active with half a dozen metal medals jingling from his tunic, though it is important to show his status in the awards he has received. To obviate the jingling of many medals the wearer can, if he wishes, have them mounted in what is known as Royal Style. Here the medals are mounted against a firm background, and though the style is a little cumbersome it has great advantages when large numbers of medals, closely overlapped, have to be worn. It also has the advantage of protecting medals on which there is some enamel in the design from becoming chipped.

The practice of wearing the complete riband and medal in miniature form is allowed, ostensibly for evening wear on special occasions.

Decorations, to use their proper title, have in certain instances the name of the recipient engraved or stamped on them, a practice that goes back to the origins cited above. A collector of such decorations has therefore not only an interest in the campaign for which the decoration was awarded, but also in the personal history of the man or woman who was so decorated. Bars or clasps are often added to a campaign medal for specified actions in which the recipient took part. Obviously the engraving of a medal with the name of a person to whom it was never awarded, of the addition of a bar or clasp to which the wearer, real or imaginary, was never entitled are pitfalls for which the collector must be on his guard.

The military history of the recipient, much of the sort of man he was, where he travelled in the service of his country, and in what actions he took part, can all be read from the medal itself, the muster rolls, mostly kept by regiments, and the history of the period in which the action took place. These medal rolls and histories serve to authenticate a medal award and are thus the collector's insurance that the man whose name is on the medal was in fact entitled to the award.

The colours of the various medal ribands are in themselves a type of heraldic representation. They are intended to convey something of the background against which the award was devised.

'The man behind the medal' becomes a very real being to

the war medal collector. So much so that there are those among medal collectors who value a well worn medal, with a faded riband, as a personal link with the man to whom it was awarded. Others, who have an eye for the colourfulness of a collection, have the medal cleaned up and a new riband fitted.

There are strong feelings among collectors on both sides of this question. In some of our cathedrals and churches there hang the banners that were carried before an army in some historic battle of long ago. Such regimental colours were laid up in these sacred places as a record, and out of respect for those who followed them. With the passing of centuries their fabric has become reduced to a spiderweb of fibres, their colours have long since departed. Should such banners be repaired? The Royal School of Needlework can restore to them all their former glory. Another century and there will be nothing left anyway. To carry out such repairs would be to destroy something indefinable; something that continues to exist by its very absence. As well might one repair the armour of the Black Prince with fibreglass panels. Yet, not to carry out such repairs is soon to lose the whole. So with the collector and his medals. The choice must be his alone.

Unusual groups of medals are of particular interest to the keen collector. They often tell the story of a man who served his country in places far apart in time and distance, in unexpected ways and for long forgotten reasons. Here again the man behind the medal is vividly with the collector, unless he be one who only collects for acquisition's sake.

From the supreme award for gallantry, the Victoria Cross, to the most humble long service and good conduct medal, what stories lie before the collector of the heroism and devotion to duty of his fellow men. Nor is the award of such medals confined only to those who face the enemy, or serve the colours. The recently instituted George Cross heads a long line of awards for bravery, devotion to duty, and service, which is thus recognised in times of both war and peace. There is probably no more cold-blooded courage in the world than that shown by those volunteers who ride out the storm in little cockleshells of lifeboats to rescue others in peril on the sea: than those volunteers who descend miles underground, surrounded by the dangers of explosion, flooding and roof collapse to rescue their fellows trapped in some mine disaster: or of those, born of our own age, who dismantle the still discovered unexploded bombs. Such courage, and much other like it, also gains its medallic reward. Here again the man behind the medal is vividly with us. For the man who, perhaps in a blaze of glory, earns the V.C. to the non-swimmer who dives into the river to rescue a doomed child, the medal is there. By it, his action is recorded for all time. On whatever line of specialisation the collector may embark, the man behind the medal is with him always.

As a conclusion, a word about the Orders of Chivalry and about Civil Decorations. These again are a field in themselves.

In some cases the Orders of Chivalry are not available for collection. Many of them must be returned to the authority which grants them, on the death of the recipient or of his closest surviving relatives.

From the Most Noble Order of the Garter: whose origins are obscure and probably not connected with the popular story: to the more humble mayoral or magistrate's badge, these are awards and badges for civil service, for services to the body politic. The great and historic Orders of Chivalry, the supreme awards, naturally stand alone in a class apart. They are granted to the favoured few, for signal service. They frequently consist of a neck badge, on a riband or a sash of riband, worn across the breast together with a breast star or other badge of rank. In the case of the Garter, an actual formalised garter forms part of the insignia. It bears the historic motto, *HONI SOIT QUI MAL Y PENSE*, and its wearing necessitates 'court dress'.

In other cases the neck collar consists of an elaborate gold chain, frequently composed of heraldic animals, lettering, and so forth. Most of them are elaborate examples of the enameller's art. Some recipients have specially made insignia, more richly encrusted than the normal award. Others, like the late Duke of Wellington, are awarded specially valuable insignia, an additional compliment for outstanding service and merit.

These Most Noble Orders of Chivalry, some of which had their origins in an act of chivalry long ago, are most closely guarded. To say that their linial descendants are such insignia as the mayoral or magistrate's badge is not strictly true. Such things as insignia of office are frequently granted automatically to the office holder, but they are no less proudly worn. There is a family tree of sorts behind them all, and there are few countries of the world who do not make some such series of civil awards and insignia of office.

All this leaves aside yet another class of medal, that awarded for some academic achievement, such as the medals granted by the Royal and British Numismatic Societies and by many such organisations, and such as those awarded for some sporting achievement. These awards are as highly personal to the recipient as are other awards but, save in a few cases, they excite little interest among collectors. There are stories of achievement behind them too, though in many cases they represent something that the recipient set out to achieve, knowing what the reward would be. They are no less significant in the scheme of medals and awards, but their interest to the collector is as yet of the slightest. Even so a phase of collecting such awards may well arise. One man at least is known who will collect any medal awarded to members of a football cup tie team though, naturally, there are not many such medals to be had.

CHAPTER ELEVEN

Token Coinage
A series on its own

There still remains something to be said about a phase of numismatics that has not so far received more than a brief reference. This particular facet of the subject concerns token coinage.

Something of the origin and purpose of tokens was mentioned in the quotation from Charlton's catalogue of Canadian coinages and their origins. Very broadly, tokens are local or private issues of pieces which stand in the place of legal coinage, and supply some deficiency in the coinage of a country. This was their origin, but such tokens are with us still in various forms.

In some domestic shops the purchaser is given stamped pieces of metal by way of rebate on the total sum spent on goods. Such pieces can often be set against the value of some

59 A typical group of Seventeenth Century Tokens; round, octagonal and heart-shaped. **60** A group of Eighteenth Century Tokens in the 'London Buildings' series. On the left are two typical obverse types. The reverses show, Goldsmiths Hall, as rebuilt after the Great Fire of London, 1666, the Royal Exchange of 1669, conceived by Thomas Gresham and long since demolished; Wren's Monument to the Great Fire (he had ideas that the column might be used as a telescope: shades of Jodrell Bank!), and the Tower of London (not so unlike the fortress shown on the medallion of Constantius Chlorus?). **61** The Cornish Penny token of the Nineteenth Century series. Note the Watt beam engine on the obverse, used for driving the pumps to keep water out of the workings. Such a wood and iron engine can be seen, often working, in the Science Museum, London. The little shapes of the reverse on either side of the fish are blocks of tin, and copper, then, with fishing, the staple products of Cornwall

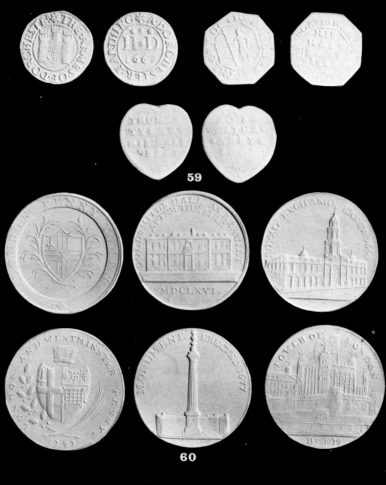

59

60

61

62   63

64

65

66

later purchase either at the same shop or at another in the chain of shops owned by the same company. Some traders offer printed paper coupons or stamps, which can be collected and used to obtain so-called gifts. All such things are related one way or another to the original traders' tokens which, so far as this country is concerned, can be said to have had their origin in a deficiency among the denominations of coins issued legally by the government.

Legal money is in itself only a token: a promise to pay, to redeem in goods. When price structures change or, to put it more simply, when the cost of living changes and there are no legal coins available to meet such a change, token coins privately issued are liable to come into being.

In Britain traders' tokens came into use in large numbers in the seventeenth century. Their definition and the reason for their appearance is set down in Williamson's two volume catalogue, *Trade Tokens Issued in the Seventeenth Century*, published in 1899. They are summed up in the following quotation from the Introduction:

'Traders' tokens formed an illegal "money of necessity", and were issued in England, Wales, and Ireland in the seventeenth century. They were the small change of the period, and were extremely useful to the people who issued and used them. They would never have been issued but for the indifference of a Government to a public need, and their issue forms a remarkable instance of a people supplying their own needs by an illegal issue of coinage, and in this way

62 'The majority of these are Spanish Eight Reale coins.' A 5s. token made from one such piece for the Deanston Cotton Mill. The figure 3 has been partly obliterated by what appears to be part of the head of George III. The basic coin was therefore probably first countermarked by the Bank of England, as mentioned in the text, for use as one of their tokens for 4s. 9d. **63** A similar piece for Cromford, Derbyshire, countermarked for 4s. 9d. **64** One of the large number of Nineteenth Century silver tokens. **65** South Eastern and Chatham Railway uniface bronze token or ticket, issued at Blackfriars Station. **66** Sheffield & Rotherham Railway bronze omnibus check.

forcing the legislature to comply with demands and requests at once just and imperative.

'Tokens are essentially democratic; they were issued by the people, and it is of the people that they speak. They record, with few exceptions, the names of no monarchs; they speak of no wars or events of great Parliamentary importance; they were not issued by Governments or Cabinets, nor by Peers or Members of Parliament, but by the unknown and small traders of well-nigh every village and town in the country, and by officials such as Mayors, Portreeves, Chamberlains, Overseers, and Churchwardens in boroughs, villages, and districts, as well as in large towns, parishes, and hundreds. The reason for their issue was to supply a public need, and when that need had been recognised by the Government and steps taken to supply it, the issue of tokens ceased, and they passed from the exchange of the shop and the market into the cabinets of the numismatist. The issue commenced in 1648 and only extended to 1679, so that the entire series forms one very short chapter of thirty years in the history of that most troublous of times in our country's history, that immediately following the execution of King Charles I. The want of small change had, however, been seriously felt in England for a long time preceding their issue. It had been considered beneath the dignity of the sovereign to issue coins of any metal baser than silver, and owing to the increased value of silver the unit of currency had become more and more minute in size and consequently inconvenient for use.'

Thus there came into being the seventeenth century series of tokens, which, though short-lived were large in numbers, well over 12,700 different issues having been made. As denominations they consisted almost entirely of Halfpenny and Farthing pieces. Practically every one tells some little local story of its county, its town, its village, and its issuer. Thus these tokens are a rich mine of local and personal history. A great deal of this history was searched out and recorded by the team of enthusiasts who helped Williamson to prepare his catalogue of the whole series. This catalogue in itself was based on an earlier work by Boyne, but even so many more issues and varieties have been added to the Williamson catalogue since it was published. So far no later complete catalogue has been published.

The tokens themselves, small, usually round pieces of copper, were unpretentious in their appearance. As a variation from the norm, some minority of pieces were octagonal or shaped like a heart. They usually had on them the name of the issuer and his type of trade or business. A good example might well be taken from a token issued in London, in Lombard Street by one, William Smith. Smith owned a tavern, the Royal Oak. The oak referred to is that in which the future Charles II hid when making his escape to the Continent after the second battle of Worcester. As this had taken place on September 3, 1651, it was an event so recent that the allusion was understood by all.

Round the edge of his token Smith had his name: *WILLIAM SMITH 1666*. In the centre the oak tree was shown, with three crowns hanging on it. There are still many inns called the 'Three Crowns', from the same period in history. On the reverse the outer legend read *IN LUMBER STREETE*, while in the middle were the words *HIS HALF PENY*.

The year 1666 was a fateful one for London, the year when a large part of it was burned down. The diarist, Samuel Pepys, who from his post in the Navy Office chronicled so much contemporary history, records that he visited the Royal Oak on April 10, 1663. He spells it 'Royall Oake Taverne, in Lumbarde Streete'. He was there again on February 18, 1664, apparently attending what would now be known as a 'business lunch'.

This little instance shows that there is almost no end to the interesting history attached to this series of tokens. Not so much detail is known about the issuers of the greater part of the series. It therefore often happens that people who take up collecting seventeenth century tokens, either as a whole, or by specialising in those of one town or county, delve into the old records of the time. Frequently such research brings to light similar interesting little stories, either about the place of issue, about the issuer himself, or about some of his contemporaries. The series as a whole, therefore, is one richly rewarding to those of an antiquarian turn of mind and to those interested in local parish, town or county history. They are relatively inexpensive to collect, but, like any series, have their rarities.

One particular point about the series makes it of interest to the collector of legal British coins. Since the authorities would not provide currency coins of small values in any quantity and of a size that could be conveniently handled in day-to-day transactions, they had to tolerate these tokens. As a result they came very close to being officially recognised. Many collectors therefore look upon them as acceptable in their cabinets of British coins.

In the next century came a further series, usually referred to as the eighteenth century tokens. The authorities still failed to issue any quantity of minor currency in copper. The demand for such a coinage became so great in 1717 that Sir Isaac Newton, then Master of the Mint, placed a contract for suitable copper fillets, rolled to the correct thickness and suitable for cutting into blanks. Until this period such copper pieces as had been issued were made under various unexpired private concessions and contracts, the story of which can be found in the work on copper coinage already mentioned.

Even now when the issue became official only £30,289 worth of Halfpence and Farthings were struck between 1717 and 1727 (George I). The inadequacy of the issue may perhaps be judged from what Matthew Boulton wrote in 1789, when he in his turn was campaigning for a proper coinage in copper. He says, 'In the course of my journeys I observe that I receive upon an average two-thirds counterfeit halfpence for change at tollgates, etc., and I believe the evil is daily increasing as the spurious money is carried into circulation by the lowest class of manufacturers who pay with it the principal part of the wages of the poor people they employ.' So, once again private issues appeared. It has been shown above that by the eighteenth century minting processes in general and minting machinery in particular had been improved, mainly by Boulton himself. The tokens now issued were pieces of larger size, about the same as that of the present Halfpennies and Pennies. They were mostly struck in copper, and many of them attained quite high artistic merit.

A very large number of the pieces put into local circulation showed buildings, some of which are still standing today but many of which have been demolished. There is a very large series usually known as 'London Buildings', which are of great interest in this respect, as well as being particularly good examples of token making at its best. They show such buildings as St Paul's Cathedral, the Mansion House, the Bank of England as it then appeared, the City gates, which still stood, and similar places of interest. The original Coventry Cathedral, St Michael's, survives on one of the series of tokens belonging to that town, as do some of its City gates and other buildings of local importance.

There are also a large number of these tokens, coming in part into the London series but with many examples to be found in other parts of the country, showing birds and animals. The 'zoological collector' is therefore quite well served. Early industrial machinery appears on some tokens, such things as water-driven drop-hammers and the famous Inclined Plane at Ketley. Our ancestors were proud of their primitive machinery, which has lead to our automated production lines, and frequently showed it in action on their tokens. Many tokens contain references to political feelings of the period: in some cases to the 'colour question', though not quite in its present context; while famous persons, real or imaginary, abound. Little or nothing of interest at this period escaped the eye of the token maker.

This series was not used in place of actual money in quite the same manner as was the seventeenth century series of tokens. Many students of the series consider that some of the pieces served little purpose than that of advertisement. Their interest therefore tends to centre more on their subject and their recording of contemporary scenes and history.

The series of copper tokens, both private and municipal, continued on into the nineteenth century. Here again the industrial revolution's rumblings are heard, in a number of pieces showing such things as early steam pumping machinery, as used in the Cornish mines. Some of Watt's famous beam engines, installed by William Murdoch (the inventor of gas lighting) when he was a young engineer in the employ of Boulton and Watt, appear on a series of Cornish pennies. Visitors to that county will be familiar with the many ruined engine houses that litter parts of the countryside. Here they are, shown in full use, on contemporary tokens. Some early industrial light railways also appear, but something of the history of trunk railway building is told at and after the same period by many commemorative medals, referred to in an earlier chapter.

The private tokens issued in the nineteenth century are not quite so prolific as were those of the eighteenth century, but the growth of the industrial revolution made its mark in an entirely different series of pieces. These are a range of countermarked coins, issued in most cases by local manufacturers for the payment of their workers. In some cases such pieces could only be cashed at a local 'Tommy shop', sponsored or owned by the manufacturer himself. This fact, with its many attendant evils, led eventually to the Truck Acts of 1831 and 1887. These countermarked token pieces no doubt played their part in bringing about the passing of the Act.

The majority of these most interesting pieces are Spanish

Eight Reale coins, overstamped with the name of the firm and a value, 4s. 9d. and 5s. being common denominations. In part the issue of such countermarked pieces no doubt arose from the shortage of actual coin provided by the Royal Mint. Reference has been made to this previously, and to the Dollars that were issued by the Bank of England to help to overcome the shortage. In making their own tokens many local manufacturers probably took the idea from the Bank. The monetary situation that arose at this time is but another illustration of the importance of a stable coinage, produced in sufficient quantity to meet national needs. It also indicates the need for very firm monetary legislation, not only against direct forgery but also against the issue and use of anything strongly resembling a coin in current use. It is an odd reflection on this particular period in our history that while actual coins were in short supply, it was easy enough to buy large quantities of Spanish Eight Reale pieces on the bullion market and put them into use in various forms. The complete history of this remarkable coin and all the various uses to which it was put throughout the world would fill a book of several volumes.

There was also yet another series of nineteenth century tokens, issued in silver, both privately and by municipalities. This series is usually known as the 'Nineteenth Century Silver Tokens'. Banks in the Channel Islands, the Isle of Man, and the municipality of the City of Bath were all notable issuers of these pieces. Many of them were well engraved and struck. A large number of them, especially those of crown size, are struck on flans obtained from the everlasting 'Spanish Dollar', and from smaller pieces in the same nation's series of coins. Many of them, and many of the privately countermarked pieces mentioned above, are now rare.

As national, inter-urban and urban transport began to develop in the form of railways, tramways and horse bus services, a series of tokens, usually used as tickets before the paper ticket came into use, began to appear in Britain, Europe and North America. Usually classified as 'transport tokens', these pieces are of great interest to anyone who studies transport development and similar allied sociological subjects. The use of such pieces continues even today in some transport undertakings.

In this country the series started with some for the original tramway, Train's first 'street railway' from Marble Arch along the Bayswater Road. Pieces appeared in many shapes and sizes, and often show the early vehicles in use for public transport at the time. Horse buses and trams, early steam and electric tramway vehicles and even early motor buses may all be found on these tokens. When 'plastics' such as celluloid, came into use, transport tokens were made from such materials. Here advantage was often taken of the fact that the tokens could be made in different colours according to face value. As a whole most of the pieces represented small amounts, usually a few pence only, some indeed being for a Halfpenny. Of the plastic pieces large issuers, among many others, were the London County Council and Birmingham Corporation tramways.

In Paris aluminium tokens were issued by the municipal tramway, showing the type of electric cars in use. Many of the continental light railway type of inter-urban tramways issued tokens in this transport series. Since both British municipal tramways and continental light railway tramways are now largely things of the past, this series of token pieces forms a most interesting sidelight on the history of public transport development. In Britain electric street tramways have vanished, apart from Blackpool where they have a specialised service to perform along the miles of sea front, but on the continent they are still very popular. This is witnessed by the fine service of modern tramcars in use in Amsterdam, in other cities of the Netherlands, and in Germany.

Unfortunately the use of local metal and plastic tickets has almost completely vanished, but in America the Token and Medal Society, TAMS for short, has devoted considerable study to this part of numismatic history and devote considerable space to the subject in their magazine. From the same part of the world also have come at least two very good catalogues. Stimulated by such activities, as well as by the relative cheapness of the tokens, there are an increasing number of collectors taking an interest in this reflection of the growth of public transport, and all that such prolific and cheap means of travel has meant to the development of modern life and social conditions. In the twentieth century the growth of the motor car, 'personal transport' as official jargon now has it, opened a new phase in transport history; one which will have even more far reaching effect on social conditions than did the once popular national and municipal transport systems. This phase is, however, largely passing unrecorded in the field of numismatics.

CHAPTER TWELVE

Numismatic Literature

The collector's backbone is his reference book. The thousands of millions of coins that have been struck over the last 20 centuries obviously need works of reference. No one can venture into this numismatic jungle without a guide.

There are guides in plenty. This book has laid special stress on the coins that were struck not more than about 164 years ago, since it is coins of this sort which have started many a collection. Even so we have tackled a section of coinage which, numerically speaking, deals with many millions of coins. Readers who have followed so far will have seen that from the turn of the 19th century improved mechanical methods of coin production have led to a vast increase in the numbers of coins struck, as has modern economic life led to a greater demand for them. The miscellaneous handful of coins that may have started our interest represents in itself a minor picture of the millions of coins which pour out every day from the mints of the world. Fortunately there are adventurers who went before us. The paths through the numismatic jungle are many, and guides multiply year by year.

An increasing number of writers have turned their interests to the very coins which comprise a miscellaneous handful of modern issues. As a result they have produced guide books of the type the beginner needs. To look back for a moment: obviously with coins being produced for some 20 centuries there can be no complete, two volume reference work dealing with the whole subject. The more or less

138

complete guide to the coins of the whole world issued over so long a period comprises a library of volumes; a library that is still growing.

The beginner's section of this large library contains many useful volumes, some few of which are listed in the bibliography. Our purpose here is to mention one or two which attempt to act as useful guides to modern coins as a whole, or to sections of modern coinage.

One which commands our attention at once, and from which we have already quoted, is an American publication, readily available in Britain, entitled the *Catalog of Modern World Coins*. Compressed within its 500 pages is a potted catalogue, with brief historical notes, of the coins of the world issued over about the last 100 years. Fully illustrated and with approximate values in U.S.A. dollars, this book is a help to the collector of modern issues in the early stages of his collecting career. Its main usefulness is in the identification of modern coins, and with it a miscellaneous handful can be broken down into sections. New editions keep the work up to date, these being published at reasonable intervals.

Having used such a book for the main breakdown of modern coins, the beginner can look around for others of a somewhat similar type which will help with the various sections into which the coins have now fallen. Reference to the bibliography is now recommended, but a few of the more general guides can be mentioned here.

Still looking at the subject on a world basis, *Gold Coins of the World*, an American publication similar to the above in its format, sorts out any gold pieces. The *Standard Catalogue of British Coins, British Copper Coins and Their Values*, and the *Milled Coinage of England* help to break up the sections still further. The *Coins of the British World* helps to sort out both British and British Empire and Commonwealth issues. All these books may be considered as basic guides. Many similar exist for the various countries of the world. The beginner will soon find one which will deal with his own particular interest, once this has been decided.

This again brings once more a point of departure, since it cannot be known along which of many lines of interest the reader may wish to specialise. General and specialised works of reference are included in the bibliography. From this it may be seen that whatever line of interest is being followed there is probably a general or specialised reference work available.

There are also a number of periodicals which need to be considered. Such periodicals try to cater for the interests of collectors in general, apart from the journals of the leading societies, which record their specialised transactions.

In this latter field the Royal Numismatic Society publish the Numismatic Chronicle annually while the British Numismatic Society publish their transactions in the British Numismatic Journal, also an annual. These journals are normally only available to Fellows and Members, and contain Papers of the greatest importance. Both Societies maintain large numismatic libraries, and books may be borrowed from them by members.

Of commercial magazines, there exists but one in Britain at the moment. This is a new publication only just over a year old, entitled *Coins and Medals*. It caters for the interests of collectors in general and is well on its way to achieving a very large world-wide circulation.

Three other magazines published in Britain are privately owned and issued to subscribers only. They are the *Numismatic Circular*, now in its seventy-fourth year, the *Coin and Medal Bulletin* and *The Numismatic Gazette*. Since they serve the dual purpose of magazine and list of numismatic material for sale, they are of interest to all collectors. On the other hand, *Coins and Medals*, through its advertisers, also offers numismatic material of all kinds.

In America, with its estimated 10 million collectors, there are a larger number of magazines as well as a weekly newspaper devoted to coins, coin collecting, and the changing picture of coin values. There are also several magazine-lists. In Europe most of the publications are society transactions, but some magazine lists are published at regular intervals. Australia has recently commenced the publication of a coin magazine.

It will be seen then that books, periodicals, and membership of a coin club, will add much to the collector's interest and can be of the greatest assistance to him whatever stage of collecting he has reached.

Select Bibliography

The following books have been selected as useful to the beginner. The length and apparently random arrangement is intended to give some idea of the great variety possible in collecting specialisation. The list is by no means complete as new books appear constantly. Older standard works are also being reprinted. Preference has been given to books in the English language and to books in print, so far as is known, at the time of going to press.

For the benefit of any reader who may have been attracted to the Classical series of coins, even though we have only mentioned them in passing, a few of the smaller standard works have been included.

GREEK SERIES

HEAD, B. V. *A Guide to the Principal Coins of the Greeks.* 1959.
Based on the very complete series of Greek coins in the British Museum.

HEAD, B. V. *Historia Numorum, a manual of Greek Numismatics.* 1911/1963.
One of the most useful one-volume works on the series.

JENKINS, G. K. and LEWIS, R. B. *Carthaginian Gold and Electrum Coins.* 1963.
A specialised work on a particular sub-series of Classical coins struck in these two metals. Electrum is a natural blend of gold and silver.

NEWELL, E. T. *Royal Greek Portrait Coins.* 1937/1963.
Another section of the Greek series in which some collectors specialise.

Select Bibliography

SELTMAN, C. T. *Greek Coins.* 1960.
Probably the best one-volume introduction to the whole Greek series.

SELTMAN, C. T. *Masterpieces of Greek Coinage.* 1949.
Emphasises the beauty of Greek coins by excellent enlarged photographs of a selection of the finer pieces.

ROMAN AND BYZANTINE SERIES

BARROWS, R. H. *The Romans.* 1961.
Not about coins but about the Romans themselves. For further reading.

GOODACRE, H. *A Handbook of the Coinage of the Byzantine Empire.* 1964.
Several times reprinted. Somewhat dated, but still a useful guide, with racy comments on Byzantine rulers and history.

GRANT, M. *The World of Rome.* 1960.
A further book about the Romans; for background reading.

HILL, SIR G. F. *Becker the Counterfeiter.* 1965 edition.
A well-told story of one of the world's most amazing forgers of rare coins. The illustrations are a protection to the collector.

KLAWANS, Z. H. *Reading and Dating Roman Imperial Coins.* 1959.
A useful American short guide to help with the problems of identification.

MATTINGLY, H. *Roman Coins, from the earliest times to the fall of the Western Empire.* 1962 edition.
Probably the best one-volume introduction to the series.

RICE, D. T. *The Byzantines.* 1962.
Background reading for the Byzantine period.

SEAR, D. R. *Roman Coins and their values.* 1964.
Another useful quick guide for the beginner.

SYDENHAM, E. A. *The Coinage of the Roman Republic.* 1952.
The standard one-volume work on the Republican series.

GENERAL WORKS

ALLEN, J. J. CULLIMORE. *The History of the British Sovereign.* 1965.
The most complete work on this particular coin. Details include the numbers struck and/or issued, and specimens struck by the Branch Mints.

BECKER, T. W. *Art in Commemorative Coins.* 1962.

BRESSETT, K. E. *A Guide Book of English Coins.* 1964.
A very useful American quick reference to the coins of the 19th and 20th century series.

BRETON, P. N. *Popular Illustrated Guide to Canadian Coins, Medals (etc.).*
A reprint of two older books, but still the most complete work as a catalogue of the series without, of course, the most recent issues.

BROOKE, G. C. *English Coins.* 1962.
The standard one-volume work on the whole of the English series, but for the somewhat more advanced collector.

BROWN, M. R. and DUNN, J. W. *A Guide to the Grading of United States Coins.* 1964.

CARSON, R. A. G. *Coins, ancient, mediaeval and modern.* 1962.
One of the most comprehensive single volume works on world numismatics ever attempted.

CHARLTON, J. E. *Standard Catalogue of Canadian Coins, Tokens and Paper Money.* 1965.
The annual standard catalogue of the Canadian series.

CLAIN-STEPHANELLI, E. E. *Russian Gold Coins.* 1962.
A good concise working catalogue, text in English.

CRAIG, W. G. *Germanic Coinages.* 1954.

CLARKE, R. L. *Catalog of the Coins of British Oceania.* 1964.
Covers modern coins of Australia, New Zealand, Fiji, etc.

COOLE, A. B. *Coins in China's History.* 1963.
A very comprehensive work which simplifies a complex series.

CROGHAN, J. R. *Canadian Cent Varieties.* 1963.
Deals with the many minor varieties of one particular denomination.

DOLLEY, R. H. M. *Anglo-Saxon Pennies.* 1964.
The most concise and readable introduction to a complex series so far published.

DUVEEN, SIR G., and STRIDE, H. G. *The History of the Gold Sovereign.* 1962.
A further book on this important coin. Deals with the original hammered series and with modern issues, but not in detail with Branch Mint issues.

FRIEDBERG, R. *Gold Coins of the World, complete from 600 A.D. to 1958.*
Very comprehensive, fully illustrated, very brief details, valuations in American dollars.

67 ABOVE: Allied to maps, time charts, historical pictures and the like, coins can be brought to life. A method in use for displaying coins in the Stockholm Cabinet. These cases show Swedish monetary history through the ages, the story being told in gold lettering embossed on leather, placed above the frame. Throughout the Stockholm Cabinet every effort is made to display coins in such a way that they attract. Visitors are not fatigued by having to stoop, lean over horizontal cases or fight against a back-reflection from badly designed lighting. It is worth a trip to Stockholm to see what *can* be done with a little imagination to make coins attractive. The museums of Britain lag far behind in exploring such possibilities for their collections of coins. (Photograph supplied. Courtesy Royal Coin Cabinet, Stockholm). 68 BELOW: Heberden Coin Room, Ashmolean Museum, Oxford, a further fine display of coins and medals.

69 The 'picture medal' at its best. The hollow bronze box, shown in the middle, opens to disclose ten charming acquatints in full colour. These depict the major naval engagements of Lord Nelson, whose portrait appears on the lid of the box. (Photograph supplied. Courtesy Spink & Son)

Select Bibliography

FRIEDBERG, R. *Coins of the British World, complete from 500 A.D. to the present.*
A similar work, fully illustrated, and with valuations in American Dollars. Both these books are very useful for primary identification of the various series which they cover.

JUDD, J. H. *United States Pattern, Experimental and Trial Pieces.* 1962.

KADMAN, L. *Israel's Money.* 1963.

KAPLAN, A. *The Coins of South Africa.* 1962.
The standard collector's catalogue of modern South African issues.

LINECAR, H. W. A. (Editor). *The Milled Coinage of England. 1662–1946.*
Standard catalogues of English gold and silver coins from Charles II to George VI. All main types illustrated, gives comparative rarity but no valuations.

LINECAR, H. W. A. *Coins.* 2nd edition. 1962.
Introductory. Gives some history, and lists the issues of coins in England, Scotland and Ireland. A general work in the Practical Handbooks for Collectors series of Ernest Benn, Ltd.

LINECAR, H. W. A. *British Commonwealth Coinage.* 1959.
Introductory. Gives tentative lists of the coins issued year by year for the countries of the Commonwealth, with some history of the territories.

LINECAR, H. W. A. *The Crown Pieces of Great Britain and the British Commonwealth.* 1962.
The only book listing serially and by main types the crown size pieces of England, Scotland and the British Commonwealth of Nations.

LOYN, H. R. *Anglo-Saxon England and the Norman Conquest.* 1962.
An important book for further reading.

LE MAY, R. *The Coinage of Siam.* 1961.
A reprint of the standard work on this series.

MACK, R. P. *The Coinage of Ancient Britain.* 2nd edition. 1964.
Deals with the very early tribal issues of Britain.

METCALF, DR. D. M. *The Coinage of South Germany in the Thirteenth Century.* 1961.
An advanced work on the complex early Germanic series.

MISHLER, C. *United States and Canadian Commemorative Medals and Tokens.* 1961.

NELSON, P. *The Coinage of William Wood.* 1722–1733.
The history of some Irish, Manx and other coins, some of which
were used in early America. With valuations.

NORTH, J. J. *English Hammered Coinage.* 2 volumes.
The latest complete work on English coins from *circa* 650 to the
reign of Charles II when milled coinage was finally introduced.
Numbered serially throughout. An advanced work, but the
standard for those interested in this series. Simplifies them as
far as possible, and gives copious historical notes.

NEWCOMB, H. R. *United States Copper Cents, 1816–1857.*
The most detailed work on this section of United States coinage.

SPINK & SON. *Catalogue of Papal Medals.* 1962.
A reprint of an earlier work. The best small guide to an interesting series of medals.

PARSONS, H. A. *The Colonial Coinages of British Africa, with the
adjacent islands.* 1950.
Deals with the African issues of colonial times, with date lists
of issues and historical notes.

PRIDMORE, CAPTAIN F. *The Coins of the British Commonwealth of
Nations to the end of the reign of George VI.*
Vol. 1. European Territories.
Vol. 2. Asian Territories, excluding India.
Vol. 3. The West Indies.
The first three parts of an exhaustive catalogue which will eventu-
ally cover all coins issued in the British Commonwealth. Fully
illustrated, every known piece catalogued, with full historical
notes.

PURVEY, F. *Collecting Coins.* 1962.
A useful beginner's book of general interest.

QUIGGIN, A. H. *A Survey of Primitive Money.* 1964.
The standard work on 'curious currency', fully illustrated, some
in colour, with complete historical notes and references.

RUDY, W. A. *Commemorative Coins of the United States.*
Catalogues the many U.S. pieces, with the history of the events
commemorated. Illustrated.

SCHOLTEN, C. *The Coins of the Dutch Overseas Territories, 1953.*
The complete catalogue of this series, covering the Dutch East
India Company pieces. Text in English or Dutch.

SANDHAM, A. *Coins, Tokens and Medals of the Dominion of Canada.*

Select Bibliography

SEABY, B. A. LTD. *Standard Catalogue of British Coins*, 1964–1965 editions.
The best pocket guide to the whole series, illustrates main types and gives valuations.

SEABY, B. A. LTD. *British Copper Coins and their values*. 1963.
As last above.

SEVERIN, H. M. *Gold and Platinum Coinage of Imperial Russia. 1701 to 1911.*
The working catalogue of this series. Text in English.

SEVERIN, H. M. *The Silver Coinage of Imperial Russia*. 1965.
As above.

SHAW, MISS E. M. *A History of Currency in South Africa*. 1956.
The complete story of the coins of this area. Illustrated.

SHAFER, N. *United States Territorial Coinage for the Philippine Islands*. 1961.

STEWART, I. H. *The Scottish Coinage*. 1955.
The best one-volume work on the history of the separate coinage of Scotland which terminated with Queen Anne.

STRIDE, H. G. *The Royal Mint, an outline history*. 1960.
The story of the Tower Hill mint by a former Chief Clerk.

TAYLOR, H. C., SOMER JAMES, and GERBINSKY, N. *The Guide Book of Canadian Coins, Currency and Tokens:* with, *The Guide Book of Great Britain's Modern Coins.*
A good pocket guide to both series, illustrated and with valuations.

TAXEY, D. *Counterfeit, Mis-struck and Unofficial U.S. Coins.*

THOMPSON, J. D. A. *Inventory of British Coins Hoards. 660–1500.* 1956.
Deals with finds of coins in Britain, illustrated and with historical notes.

WAYTE RAYMOND. *The Silver Dollars of North and South America.* Revised and reprinted, 1964.
Dollar and crown size coins are a great favourite with most collectors. Works dealing with them are always welcome.

DAVENPORT, DR. J. *European Crowns and Talers since 1800.* 1964. European Crowns, 1700–1800, 1965. German Talers 1700–1800, 1965. The standard set of books for the European crown-size collector. Fully illustrated and with valuations.

YEOMAN, R. S. *Catalog of Modern World Coins.* 6th edition.
Probably the best one-volume work to help with the classification of modern world coins as a whole. Fully illustrated, with

brief historical notes and valuations. New editions appear, bringing the book up to date, about every two years.

FOR THE MEDAL COLLECTOR

There are many books dealing with decorations and medals, civil awards and so forth. Quite a few of them concern the decorations of their own particular country. They are, therefore, in the language of that country, and translations are rarely available. Since almost without exception such books are very well illustrated, many with colour plates, it is not essential for the collector to know the language in which the book may be written.

BABIN, L. L. *Foreign War Medals, Decorations and Orders.*

BABIN, L. L. *Cap Badges of the Canadian Expeditionary Forces, 1914–1919.*

BABIN, L. L. *Japanese War Medals, Orders and Decorations.*
Of the above the first and third are actually dealer's lists. Since they are American publications the word 'foreign' includes Europe. They make useful reference works for the beginner, and have illustrations and valuations.

BAX, DR. W. F. *De Nederlandse Ridderorden en Onderscheidingen* 1951.
Covers medals and orders of the Netherlands.

BERGHMAN, A. *Nordiska Riddereodnar och Dekorationer.* 1949.
Covers Norway.

BELDER, B. L. *United States War Medals.* 1962.
Decorations Officielles Francaises. 1956.
A lavishly produced government official record of French medals and orders.

DORLING, H. TAPRELL. *Ribbons and Medals.*
The working catalogue for the collector. Has passed through many editions and is brought up to date about every ten years. Illustrated.

EDWARDS, T. *Regimental Badges, 1963.*

GORDON, L. L. *British Battles and Medals.* 1962.
Another working catalogue for the collector. Fully illustrated, with much history and lively comment.

HAZELTON, A. W. *The Russian Imperial Orders.*

Select Bibliography

MAYO, J. H. *Medals and Decorations of the British Army and Navy.* 1897.

Very fully illustrated. Though dated, is still a most important work for the collector. Out of print, but reasonably available at second hand. Two volumes.

MEDCALF, G.*Hawaiian Royal Orders, Insignia, Classes, Regulations and Members.* 1962.

QUINOT, H. *Recueil Illustre des Ordres de Chevalerie et Decorations Belges de 1830 a 1963.*

The standard work on Belgian medals and orders.

SAWICKI, J. A. *Nazi Decorations and Medals, 1933–1945.*

Covers a subject on which many collectors specialise, and in which there is plenty of collector's material available.

SMYTH, SIR JOHN. *The Story of the Victoria Cross, 1856–1963.*

TANCRED, G.*Historical Record of Medals and Honorary Distinctions conferred on the British Navy, Army and Auxiliary Forces, 1891.*

Much the same comment as for Mayo, above.

PERIODICALS

There are not very many periodicals published in Britain at the moment which cater for the interests of coin and medal collectors. We therefore list a number of publications, some of which come from overseas, in order to give something of a picture of numismatic periodicals as a whole. Here again preference has been given to publications in the English language.

THE NUMISMATIC CHRONICLE. Published annually by the Royal Numismatic Society. This is a record of the transactions of the Society during the year. It is normally issued to Fellows of the Society only, but copies may be obtained from dealers. It covers mainly the more advanced fields of numismatic research, reviews books of importance published during the year, and is mainly devoted to the Classical series of coins: those of Ancient Greece and Rome.

THE BRITISH NUMISMATIC JOURNAL. Published annually by the British Numismatic Society, and normally only available to Members. Copies can be obtained from dealers. The British Numismatic Society concerns itself mainly with the more advanced

THE FARE BOX. General interest. From P.O. Box 1204, Boston, Mass.

problems and research of British coinage. Important books are reviewed and the transactions of the Society recorded.

COINS AND MEDALS. This is a recently founded magazine, dealing with the more popular and less specialised aspects of coin collecting. Its articles are of general interest and wide coverage. It is the only commercial magazine available 'on the bookstalls', and can be strongly recommended to the beginner and to all collectors. Published by the Link House Group, Croydon, Surrey.

THE NUMISMATIC CIRCULAR. A private publication, sent out by post to subscribers only. Founded in 1893, eleven issues are published each year. It combines articles of specialised and general interest with lists of coins and medals offered for sale to the collectors. Over the years such lists are a good indication of the values of coins on the market. Published by Spink & Son, Ltd., London, S.W.1.

THE COIN AND MEDAL BULLETIN. A similar publication to the Numismatic Circular. Published by B. A. Seaby, Ltd., London, W.1.

NEWS LETTER. Records the transactions of the London Numismatic Club, and available to members only. Contains papers of general interest, not too advanced.

THE NUMISMATIC GAZETTE. General interest. From Corbitt and Hunter, Ltd., 2 St. Nicholas Buildings, Newcastle-upon-Tyne.

AUSTRALIAN NUMISMATIC JOURNAL. Of Australian and general interest. From the National Gallery, Adelaide, South Australia.

THE AUSTRALIAN COIN REVIEW. Australian and general interest. From the Hawthorn Press, 15 Guildford Lane, Melbourne.

CALCOIN NEWS. American and general interest. From 935 Sutter Street, San Francisco, California.

CANADIAN COIN NEWS. Canadian, American and general interest. From 62 Richmond Street, W. Toronto.

THE CANADIAN NUMISMATIC JOURNAL. Official publication of the Canadian Numismatic Society, Ottawa, Ontario.

COIN GALLERIES NUMISMATIC REVIEW AND FIXED PRICE LIST. General interest. From 123 West 57th Street, New York.

COIN WORLD. General interest. From P.O. Box 150, Sidney, Ohio.

THE COLONIAL NEWSLETTER. General interest. From P.O. Box 2014, Little Rock, Arkansas, U.S.A.

Select Bibliography

THE JOURNAL OF THE TOKEN AND MEDAL SOCIETY. Tokens in general, especially transport, commemorative medals, and similar interests. From Russell Rulau, Sidney, Ohio.

NEW ZEALAND NUMISMATIC JOURNAL. The official organ of the Royal Numismatic Society of New Zealand. From P.O. Box 23, Wellington, New Zealand.

NUMISMATIC NEWS. General. From Iola, Wisconsin, U.S.A.

THE NUMISMATIC SCRAPBOOK MAGAZINE. General interest. From 7320 Milwaukee Avenue, Chicago, U.S.A.

THE NUMISMATIST. General interest. Official organ of the American Numismatic Association. From 3520 North 7th Street, Phoenix 14, Arizona.

THE WHITMAN NUMISMATIC JOURNAL. General interest. From 1220 Mound Avenue, Racine, Wisconsin, U.S.A.

WORLD COINS. General interest. From P.O. Box 150, Sidney, Ohio.

Practically all the larger European countries publish numismatic magazines, and many dealers publish magazine lists. One periodical alone lists them all, reviews what they write, and reviews all new books. This is NUMISMATIC LITERATURE, published quarterly by the American Numismatic Society, Broadway between 155th and 156th Street, New York, N.Y. 10032, U.S.A.

TOKENS

BELL, R. C. *Commercial Coins, 1787–1804.* 1963.

BELL, R. C. *Copper Commercial Coins, 1811–1819.*

DALTON, R. and HAMER, S. H. *The Provincial Token-Coinage of the Eighteenth Century.* 1910, etc.
The standard work on the series, unfortunately out of print.

DAVIS, W. J. *The Nineteenth Century Token Coinage of Great Britain, Ireland, the Channel Islands and the Isle of Man.* 1904.
The standard work on the series, unfortunately out of print.

DAVIS, W. J. and WATERS, A. W. *Tickets and Passes of Great Britain and Ireland.* 1922.
The standard work, unfortunately out of print.

MATHIAS, P. *English Trade Tokens.* 1962.

SEABY, H. A. and BUSSELL, MONICA. *British Copper Coins and their values*. 1965.
The best brief working catalogue available in the absence of the standard works. Covers not only regal issues but the 17th, 18th and 19th century tokens.

WATERS, A. W. *Notes on 18th century Tokens*. 1954.

WATERS, A. W. *Notes on the Silver Tokens of the Nineteenth Century*. 1957.

WETTON, J. L. *The Hampshire Seventeenth Century Traders' Tokens*. 1964.

WETTON, J. L. *The Isle of Wight Seventeenth Century Traders' Tokens*.

WILLIAMSON, G. C. *Trade Tokens issued in the Seventeenth Century in England, Wales and Ireland by Corporations, Merchants, Tradesmen, etc.* 2 vols. 1889.
The standard work, unfortunately out of print.

Index

Index

Russia, 77, *ill.* no. 28
Rye Coin Club, 66

St Albans Numismatic Soc., 66
St George, 75
St John (Canada), 88
Saka Era, 84
Salford Museum, 98
Samvat Era, 84
Sandwich, Earl of, 75
Sandford Saltus medal, *ill.* no. 58
Sarawak, 79, *ill.* no. 29
Scandinavia, 38
Sceatta, Anglo-Saxon, 75, *ill.* no. 14
Scotland, 34, 76 (*see also* Shilling)
Scunthorpe, 66
'Second-hand' coins, 41
Seychelles, 84–5, *ill.* no. 36
Sheffield Numismatic Soc., 67
Shilling: English, 29, 34, *ill.* no. 8; Irish, 77, *ill.* no. 18; Scottish, 29–30, 34, *ill.* no. 8
Ship designs, 75
Siam, 84
Simon, Thomas, 96
Simplon Tunnel, *ill.* no. 55
Singapore, 79
Sixpence, 30, 34; Irish, 77, *ill.* no. 18
Sloane, Sir Hans, 93, 95
Smith, William, 131
Soho Mint, 109, 112
South Africa: coins, 82, 85, 113; mint, 114
Southampton, 67
Southern Rhodesia, 81, 89, *ill.* no. 33
Sovereign (£1), 28–9, 31–3, 74, 110, *ill.* no. 5
Spanish coins, 134–5, *ill.* nos. 62–3
'Specimen' coins, 113
Stephenson, George, *ill.* no. 53
Stirling: Smith Institute, 98
Stockholm cabinet, *ill. facing* 144
Straits, Settlements, 79, 85, *ill.* no. 30

Study and research, 71–2, 92–4
Surrey, Earl of, 38
Surrey Numismatic Soc., 67
Swann, H. S., 57
Sydney Mint, 82, 86, 111, 113–14

Ten-shilling piece, 33
Tenth of a penny, *ill.* no. 43
Testoon, 34
Thaler, *ill.* no. 16
Threepence: Irish, 77, *ill.* no. 18; silver, 30–1, 35, 76, *ill.* no. 9; twelve-sided, 28, 30, 35, 61, 75–6, *ill.* no. 15
Tokens, 86–8, 98, 128–37, *ill.* nos. 59–66; silver, 135
Torbay, 117
Toronto, 88
'Trade' dollars, 74
Traders' token coins, 86, 129–35
Trafalgar Medal, *ill.* no. 56
Tramways, 135–6
Transport tokens, 136, *ill.* nos. 65–6
Treasure trove, 93
Truck Acts, 134
Turton, 58
Two-guinea piece, 33
Twopence, 30–1, 35, *ill.* no. 9
Two pounds, 33, 58, *ill. facing* 33
Two-shilling piece, *see* Florin
Tyneside Numismatic Soc., 67

Uncirculated coins, 40–1
U.S.A., *see* America
U.S.S.R., *see* Russia

'Very Fine' (V.F.) coins, 43
Victoria Cross, 125–6
Victoria, Queen, 29, 34, 80, 107, 120, *ill.* no. 44; new Jubilee coinage, 111
Vienna, 74
Vigo Bay, battle of, 97, 117–19, *ill.* no. 52
Vikrama Era, 84
Vile, William, 58

158